This Book Belongs to

ALSO BY
MEGAN MORTON
----
home ♥ love

Living and breathing everything to do with the home, Megan Morton has been called on to style, design and work her 'house whispering' powers for celebrities, magazines and her next-door neighbours. Her work has been featured on the covers of international glossies including *Elle Decoration* UK and *Vanity Fair*. Locally, her clients include *Vogue Living*, *In Style* and *Inside Out* magazines. Her column for the 'Good Weekend' magazine in the *Sydney Morning Herald* and *The Age* inspired her first book, *Home Love*. When she's not dressing homes and styling mantelpieces, Megan works creating 'luxury atmospheres' for special occasions and dreams up beautiful rooms that make people obscenely happy. She also has a school where she teaches, along with other inspired people, the tricks of the trade – theschool.com.au.

meganmorton.com

Affectionately dedicated to all who love home.

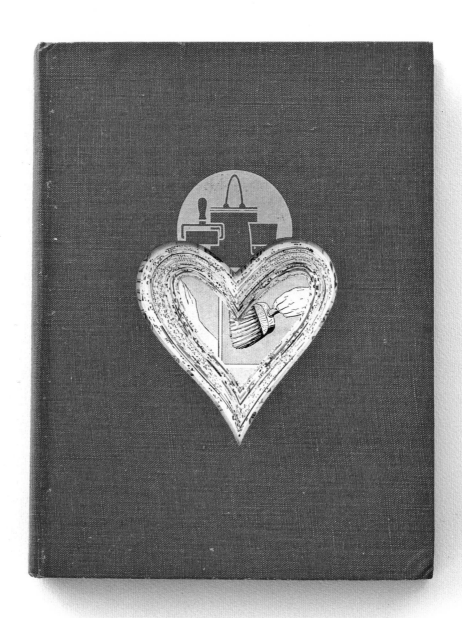

MEGAN MORTON

THINGS
I
LOVE

conran OCTOPUS

Have you ever tried
to peel a piece of fruit
in one go,
trying to keep
a steady hand and
concentrate hard to make
that curly skin?
After you've peeled and
peeled and can peel
no more, there's the skin,
all wonderful and curly.
Well, *Things I Love*
is my apple peel,
and boy is it good
to get it out
into the world!

Introduction

As an interiors stylist I work every day with a lot of beautiful things, things so beautiful that some days my eyes hurt from the sheer excess of what I've seen. But however beautiful we stylists make rooms, there are two ingredients we can't supply: interest in and love of the things in them – in other words, the human element or, more simply, *heart*.

In this book I wanted to write about the *joie de vivre* of my work as a stylist. Not a day goes by without someone asking me 'How can I be a stylist too?' But what they really want to know is not how to *be* a stylist but how to *think* like one! A good stylist is:

- ▲ a *bon vivant* but not a snob
- ● a big-picture person who's also firmly fixated on the details
- ■ someone who makes it look easy but knows all too well it isn't
- ▲ someone whose spirit matches their style
- ● someone who can be uptown one day and downtown the next, and be ready to go somewhere off the beaten track in a week.

So in the same spirit, the sections of this book swing from high to low, from knockout house-pervs (Part 1: Houses I Love) and gorgeous things (Part 2: Things I Love) to an insanely Protestant way to keep your linen cupboard in order, and other useful tips (Part 4: Things I Love to Do). You also get to mingle with some clever collaborators (Part 3: People I Love) and enjoy my Homelove Manifesto (see page 202).

What is styling anyway? To me it's a noun, a verb and an adjective:

- ▲ Styling as an *art form* is visual science.
- ● Styling as a *process* is all about sharing. A noble stylist forms symbiotic relationships and seeks out unusual partnerships that play to both parties' strengths.
- ■ Styling as a *practice* is about protecting the viewer from a space's flaws while at the same time being generous enough to celebrate its seen (and sometimes unseen) beauty.

I know all too well that a home-lover doesn't have tons of time on their hands or even enough coins in their purse, so I hope this book will tick all the boxes for all readers who love their home.

ONE

HOUSES

I LOVE

Putting together a look for your home that's as individual as you are starts with a reality check of your lifestyle and purse strings. The rest is shopping!

Home-renovation shows have turned home decoration into a spectator sport. They all make the same seductive promise – an army of experts will discover the 'house beautiful' beneath the chaotic clutter, sometimes in less than a day! But what happened to the idea of putting your own stamp on a space?

I want to share some special homes with you. Some were decorated to a strict budget, others don't know the meaning of the word. Some are quietly spoken spaces that whisper, 'Come in, it's beautiful here,' while others scream rollercoaster-crazy fun.

I love styling houses with real bite and character. You know those ones that make you want to pull the magazine apart at the spine so you can see just a smidge more? The following private spaces belong to people who are so clued up decoratively they've created spaces that inspire. All of them get homelove gold stars for being such beautiful and confident examples of personal style at home. ■

HOUSES I LOVE

NIGEL, NEW YORK.

Directors of photography (DOPs) are resolute when it comes to the quality of light. Nigel is a legend in the world of DOPs and, to facilitate his work life, has homes in many places. This weeny one, tucked away on the Lower East Side, is one of his favourites, thanks largely to the way light and dark play out in the course of a day. Deliberately dark, it provides a devastatingly handsome backdrop for some of his favourite things. Its compact floor plan allows for some genius space-saving ideas, like his loft bed. Why give over valuable floor space to the room that's used the least? Dead clever. ■

Why cheat a compact space into looking oversized? Nigel's place shows that small, dark and moody can be more powerful than light, bright and pretend big.

THE HARTES, SYDNEY.

Has a house ever found you?
That once-in-a-lifetime house that's so
fundamentally rock-solid good you just
have to live there? This is one of those
gems. Elegant, but fun, Susan truly is her
house. And it is her. Moving back from
New York with her three kids, husband
and dog, she knew this couldn't be the
one that got away. This house can really
do no wrong. All her furniture, art pieces
and objects just work. And with its green
carpet, original Marion Hall Best kitchen
and rose-pink façade, the house just sings
under Susan's harmonising influence. ■

A lot of people put artwork and important visuals up a staircase, but it's wasted given people are always on their way up or down. Enter wallpaper (in Susan's case, Josef Frank's 1940s Vårklocka design in white from justscandinavian.com) – the perfect use for busy prints. It's a no-brainer, up or down. Please be careful where you place wallpaper. It can hurt!

The Hartes' home is working with one part modern, two parts antiquities and one hundred per cent original. And it's thanks to this little recipe that their rooms are so comforting and ever so slightly quirky.

HANNAH, SYDNEY.

Carving living spaces out of diminutive floor plans is genius territory only. The way I see it, anyone can make a big chunk of space work. But those who make minimal square-metreage special are the ones to look out for. Hannah Tribe, of course, has an architectural pedigree, but she encourages small spaces to bloom just as much as her big jaw-droppers. Her own home is a study in light and modernism but also a reality check. If you have a shoebox apartment or even a matchbox (a studio!), take heed of Hannah's three-bedroom terrace. It's not how much space you've got, it's what you do with it. ∎

Black-and-white never fails, I promise. While it tempers Hannah's plywood and fibre-cement building palette perfectly, it also works wonders in older homes. But, like Hannah, don't work with half black, half white but use black as highlights on white or vice versa.

THE BARNUMS, SYDNEY.

Having spent my early years fairly isolated and defiantly not near any shops that didn't sell produce or feed supplies, I spent my time drooling over Peter Alexander PJ catalogues and listening to my Vitabeats LP. Lissa and Andrew Barnum were the Vitabeats and they were, simply put, outstanding!

Years later, I was sent to a wonderful restored church with original floorboards and steeple for *Marie Claire Lifestyle* magazine. When Lissa opened the door and I was face to face with my teenage dream, I went white. To prove my affections, I dropped my box of props and recited my most loved Vitabeats song. They had put down their keyboards and mixers and were now design academics and artists. Ten years later, thanks to Facebook, Lissa and I hooked up and I listened to Andrew's brilliant new work.

The newly re-renovated church is an involved, complicated, textured, happy house that positively hums with life. Lissa found most of her doors second-hand for twelve dollars each. Respect for reclaimed materials has become fashionable, but for Lissa and Andrew it's just the way they go about their lives. My teenage crush continues . . . ∎

The Barnums' house really has to be this way. How else would they design, write music, make art, paint and eat really well all under the one roof? They checked every door, every window, for its sustainability and environmental impact. Who wouldn't if it means a drawbridge of recycled beams linking old church to new wing?

ARI, BRISBANE.

Sunshine, sweet sunshine! I love my home state of Queensland – its architecture and people positively glow. Ari Athans is a serious jeweller, and I love her house for its charming double nature. It has one foot in the world of serious architecture, with its ingenious floor plan and clever details, but the other foot firmly in fun. It is, after all, a place where her two children and their friends run wild, from pool to terrace to playroom. A contemporary art collection presides over them all, which nicely merges both sides of the home's personality. (Yes, this book has a small bias towards Queensland: go to GOMA – the Gallery of Modern Art – in Brisbane and see what all the fuss is about.) ■

Ari's place reminds me of a Moroccan souk. It all looks very normal from the outside but then bam! It's all Ari's world from the front door onwards. Surprises can be nice.

Not every architecturally designed house makeover needs to remove all traces of character. Ari has left her bathroom as is – apart from replacing the floor tiles and splashing out on a new cupboard.

GEORGIE, SYDNEY.

Sometimes people defy category.
Sometimes they're so in tune with
what they love there's only one way to
decorate – their way! Georgie, a jeweller,
has an incredible visual mind and style –
she's the only person I know who can
reference about eight countries at
once in the one room. When you take
a closer look, you can see how she loves
to merge the intricate with the majestic.
She commissioned artisans in India and
glassblowers in Italy to make her doors
and lights, but ingeniously painted the
doors on her kitchen cupboards herself,
freehand! I know, I know. Some people,
as Lady Gaga says, are just born that way. ■

Intricate details will always draw the eye into a space. It's a stroke of genius when you're trying to add intimacy and interest to large open spaces.

HOUSES I LOVE

VANESSA, NEW YORK.

Vanessa is possibly the cleverest person in the creative universe. And like the name of her tumblrzine, she's also supernice. She shares her loft in New York with her husband Simon, her kids Yas and Harper, and a guinea pig called Fudge. Most New Yorkers sweat over their real-estate decisions (and rightly so, given a laundry is a luxury), but when Vanessa saw this loft early on, the search was over, the deal was done and it was off to the Odeon for a round of champagne and *frites*.

But it's how she's dressed it that makes it … Just. Oh. So. Wonderful! It's best described as a space that appears to be on permanent holiday, and that's the way they like to live. Messages are left up from old parties, artwork has been given by equally talented friends (clever people are always magnets for other clever people) and everywhere there's evidence of their family's relaxed aesthetic. The family is super-busy – especially Vanessa – but she'll always make time for a martini. Quick, quick, quick, it's Vanessa. Drink up and listen carefully: what she says is golden. ∎

Open-plan living is hard – you either have to be as neat as a pin or, like Vanessa, just roll with it and let life fill every corner. To keep it all together she's secured simply designed functional pieces and customised with her choice of art and trimmings.

HOUSES I LOVE

VICTUS, MELBOURNE.

In her book *The House in Good Taste*, actor and decorator Elsie de Wolfe, one of my favourite women, asks, of decorating, 'What is the goal?', then answers her own question: 'A house that is like the life that goes on within it, a house that gives us beauty as we understand it.'

This comes to mind when I'm inside Victus's enormous triple-fronted terrace. Its rooms offer comfort and every corner has something delicious, interesting and/or wonderful for the eyes to rest on. It's beauty as Victus understands it. ∎

How do you give a huge
home (a former boarding
house) focus? Introduce
a focal point is how.
Victus's is her hallway
mural by artist Julia
Gorman, yours could be
an oversized artwork,
a groaning chandelier
or a majestic mobile.

RICHARD, MONTAUK, NY.

Richard from Chandelier Creative is one of New York's VIPs in the creative field. His friends all benefit from his generosity and love of life come the weekends, when it's off to Montauk. I've never met a weekender as exciting as this. Its primary purpose is to be an adults' playground. They keep bees for honey, stoke a fire pit at night, put up teepees for extra accommodation and, come sundown, watch movies on the alfresco cinema screen. The idea is to work hard all week and play harder on the weekend. Totally inspiring. Totally homeloving. Richard Christiansen, like your Chandelier Creative website, you *are* awesome-world! ■

Weekenders are the places to play out your decorative fantasies. If your home is a mad cacophony, make your retreat restorative, John Pawson–like and single-themed. If you live in a camera-ready space, make a mad dash for it with your weekender. With his Chandelier Surf Shack, Richard has created an awesome getaway that's both totally camera-ready *and* people-ready.

HOUSES I LOVE

The Endless Summer

KIDS & CHICKENS, SOUTHERN HIGHLANDS.

Family life really does throw up a few challenges in terms of decorating a home, no matter how much or how little help you have. What I love about the Wolkensteins' home is that it's so family-friendly. All its surfaces are totally manageable and low-maintenance – concrete floors, wipe-able surfaces, almost no potential dust pits – and the general decorating style is bright, cheery and, best of all, washable. It means there's no 'good' room, or out-of-bounds area, so everyone can be together. Smart Wolkensteins! ∎

High-maintenance houses, like high-maintenance relationships, can get exhausting. The Wolkenstein house sports all the charms of its country provenance with all the low-maintenance mod cons.

BETSY, NEW YORK.

A house usually asserts its own personality before you even get inside it. I love how Betsy has dressed her house according to its DNA. The art is understanding what's possible in a house, what its true potential is, then working back towards a glorious result.

If your house were a person, who would it be? Betsy, a decorator, was working with a brownstone with major attitude – lots of heavy-duty rigorous materials and really large rooms that could easily engulf furniture. She's added major artworks, large-scale furniture pieces and every now and then a surprise, such as the chocolate backing to her library shelves or the stalactite-esque chandelier in the kitchen.

Is your house a classic knockout à la Audrey Hepburn, with all the structure required to be a classic beauty? Or is it more dishevelled, à la Carly Simon, with natural beauty but could do with a little tidy-up? Or is it more like Sophia Loren, an ageing beauty who looks best in dramatic broad brushstrokes and has little time or need for smaller accessories? I mean, can you imagine putting Sophia Loren in a loose cotton floral dress without boning or structure?

To let *your* house or apartment express its personality, look at it honestly, then make changes and improvements in character with it. Voilà! ■

Antique and modern are at play here but never at odds. Betsy can appreciate the big and the little, the old and the new – and, as her home suggests, mixing the two makes each better.

Large homes do well with a softer colour. Sometimes room upon room of white is just plain uninspired. Whisper-soft pistachio is in Betsy's office. It's Farrow and Ball's Pale Powder (not available in Australia) but quarter-strength Dulux Meadow Lane is a close match.

IVAN & MARY, NEW YORK.

Plaster: wet or dry, aged or fresh, I love the stuff. Ivan Schwartz, as part of StudioEIS, is one of the last people doing this life-sized sculptural plasterwork. Spending time in his workspace in Brooklyn, New York, is beyond inspiring. Black gaffer tape is used hilariously to disguise the warehouse walls and create a view to a mock outside. To-do lists on the office blackboard are highlighted by Christmas-light surrounds. The kitchen features a bottle-shaped corkboard made from the stoppers of wine studio visitors have enjoyed. Ivan, along with his Australian studio partner Mary van de Wiel – a brainy branding specialist and radio commentator – have so many books spanning such an exciting range of topics that I had to stop myself making piles to read between shots. Music of all genres pipes through the space. And I lost count at forty-six lamps. I could have spent days shooting their workspace. Days. Months. Years. It's that kind of place, where you can lose all track of time and temporarily inhabit the body of a highly curious version of yourself – like a ten-year-old you who knows everything you know about houses and loves what you love. That's what it's like to be in Mary and Ivan's studio – stepping back as well as oh so totally forward. ■

Part makeshift,
Ivan and Mary's
space is a lesson in
the qualities of time-
worn wood, dressed
with noblemen in
portraits and busts.
It's one part history
lesson, two parts
decoration inspiration,
where the items are
mostly made by
Ivan and Mary,
or are presents from
equally talented friends.

JULIA, MELBOURNE.

Artist Julia Ritson gets woken up by the morning sun pouring through a large-diameter round bedroom window. The sunlight makes an incredible shape in the room, becoming a stretched ellipse by day's end. This lightness upstairs counters the darkness downstairs. Julia's main concern is light and dark and all the lovely nuances in between, so her studio, with its overhead skylight, has incredibly varied a.m. and p.m. capabilities.

An architect may have designed the place for himself, but Julia and her partner, Stefan, have really made it their own. Downstairs never feels sombre, thanks to all the greenery in the adjoining garden. It always feels like gin-and-tonic o'clock, no matter the time of day! How clever is black and white? ∎

The framed text artwork reads:

ABUSE OF POWER COMES AS NO SURPRISE
ASCOLTA QUANDO IL CORPO TI PARLA
ACTION CAUSES MORE TROUBLE THAN THOUGHT
C'È UNA SOTTILE DIFFERENZA TRA INFORMAZIONE E PROPAGANDA
BOREDOM MAKES YOU DO CRAZY THINGS
DOVRESTI VIAGGIARE LEGGERO
CATEGORIZING FEAR IS CALMING
È MEGLIO ESSERE INGENUI CHE INDIFFERENTI
EATING TOO MUCH IS CRIMINAL
GLI UOMINI NON SONO MONOGAMI PER NATURA
EXPIRING FOR LOVE IS BEAUTIFUL BUT STUPID
I BAMBINI SONO LA SPERANZA DEL FUTURO
FATHERS OFTEN USE TOO MUCH FORCE
I BAMBINI SONO PIÙ CRUDELI DI TUTTI
GO ALL OUT IN ROMANCE AND LET THE CHIPS FALL WHEREVER
I DESIDERI ARTIFICIALI STANNO SACCHEGGIANDO LA TERRA
IDEALS ARE REPLACED BY CONVENTIONAL GOALS AT A CERTAIN AGE
IL DENARO CREA IL GUSTO
IF YOU AREN'T POLITICAL YOUR PERSONAL LIFE SHOULD BE EXEMPLARY
IL PECCATO È UNO STRUMENTO DI CONTROLLO SOCIALE
IT IS MAN'S FATE TO OUTSMART HIMSELF
L'AMORE INCONDIZIONATO DIMOSTRA GENEROSITÀ DI SPIRITO
IT'S A GIFT TO THE WORLD NOT TO HAVE BABIES
L'INACCESSIBILE IMMANCABILMENTE ATTRAE
LACK OF CHARISMA CAN BE FATAL
LA DISORGANIZZAZIONE È UNA SPECIE DI ANESTESIA
MOTHERS SHOULDN'T MAKE TOO MANY SACRIFICES
LA MODERAZIONE UCCIDE LO SPIRITO
PEOPLE WHO DON'T WORK WITH THEIR HANDS ARE PARASITES
LA RELIGIONE CREA TANTI PROBLEMI QUANTI NE RISOLVE
PRIVATE PROPERTY CREATED CRIME
LE PAURE ATAVICHE SONO LE PEGGIORI
RAISE BOYS AND GIRLS THE SAME WAY
OGNI SURPLUS È IMMORALE
SLOPPY THINKING GETS WORSE OVER TIME
RICORDATI CHE HAI SEMPRE LA LIBERTÀ DI SCELTA
THERE'S A FINE LINE BETWEEN INFORMATION AND PROPAGANDA
UCCIDERE È INEVITABILE MA NON BISOGNA ESSERNE FIERI
YOU ARE GUILELESS IN YOUR DREAMS
UN UNICO EVENTO PUÒ AVERE INFINITE INTERPRETAZIONI

To counterbalance having the artist's studio at home, the living space has a grown-up dignity about it. As Julia admits, it's needed as 'the calm before the painting storm'.

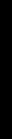

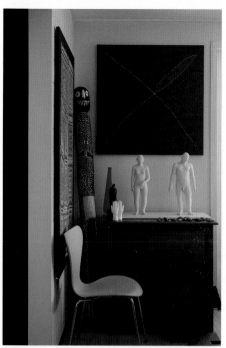

SHAN, BRISBANE.

Although Shan would hate to be called Brisbane's most stylish woman, that's the truth. She's been a fashion merchant for decades and given her two now-grown-up children a ridiculously wholesome childhood in their Brisbane home. Shan, who has a thing for fabrics, has made everything that endures high traffic and animals (they have six dogs!) washable. The fabrics, tapestries and quilts also lend the home softness and a distinct homeliness that offset her rather serious art collection to perfection.

The same applies to her penchant for quality – her Arne Jacobsen dining chairs, rather than the standard black or birch, are lolly pink and lime green. Her kitchen, though, is black (Flight Plan by British Paints), ideal for a space that needs to be the centre of the action but remain decoratively camouflaged. On her dining table you can expect to see a teapot from Cuba, a pair of gloves on a stand, a rare hat, or a book she's engaged in, rather than any pretentious flower or decorative centrepiece.

Shan knows that objects are special, and that when you see a vintage, mint-condition raffia sunhat and an African photography book, you really do want to know all about them. Her bravery with red (British Paints' Devil Cloak) has paid off handsomely, making a focal point of her tongue-and-groove walls. ■

HOUSES I LOVE

Deep red becomes the unknowing lifeblood of Shan's house. Want to hold a multitude of paintings and artworks together without it coming across all Peggy Guggenheim and museum-like? Pick a colour (it doesn't have to be red) to take the blow of it all and watch everything soften.

HOUSES I LOVE

ANNIE, SYDNEY.

Decoration is an art, a discipline where
careful balance must be maintained.
Annie Wilkes, Australia's *most* talented
landscaper, understands this. She believes
in the sky and earth, as well as plantings
and antiquities from faraway places.
Her true skill, though, is her art of living.
She can dress a space like no one else.
Her ideas are about turning things on
their head, flirting with volume and scale.
She always has more than one way to
view a problem, which gives her the edge
when it comes to solutions. Using grand
gestures, she works with the *petits soins*
of everyday life. She believes in mirror
on mirror – and why buy a bag of oranges
when you can have a wheelbarrow full?
Her interior is a refuge for her art that
works hand in glove with her magnificent
garden. Best of all, Franklyn, her ageing
pointer, has the run of the place. ∎

Humour can be a wonderful thing in a house. While Annie has impeccable taste, she can't help but show her quick wit. Fifty faux parrots crowd her desk. She has a pair of Marilyns in a totally grey-on-grey house. She's decanted four varieties of sugar into beautiful glass vessels. There are no internal doors. Anywhere. Annie shows that the only rules to live by should be your own.

HOUSES I LOVE

OUR HOUSE, SYDNEY.

People are shocked when they see that our dishwasher hasn't been built in yet. When we bought the house I thought I'd be renovating ASAP, but it's been like this for three years now. I'm far more worried about having something lovely to look at when we're all cosied up on the couch. We had aimed to knock down all but one wall and make a big architectural statement, but we soon realised this house would never produce a real Cinderella moment.

Once I'd taken down my wallpaper of photocopied plans (which distracted me from the reality and allowed me to visualise the possible), I began to see our charming little 1940s house for what it was – architecturally barren, but with a perky, petite floor plan that gave a slight sense of being on a holiday camp. It has a weeny kitchen, which I like, generous communal spaces, and kooky small rooms that my children and their friends can really live in.

A home like ours is an opportunity for vignettes, little patches of wonder to distract the eye from its barefaced flaws. So I created jubilant little moments that really mean nothing to anyone but my family. It's far from perfect but, as the sign says, 'It's beautiful here.' ∎

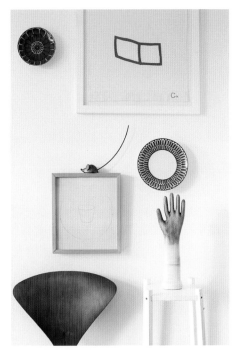

Houses don't need
to stick to one colour
palette. I painted half
my floor black and the
other half white just so
I could report back on
which is better to live
with! Accidents, though,
can turn into wonderful.
Whether your place is
fully integrated or a little
more higgledy-piggledy,
if you put something
of yourself into it, it's
a guaranteed home.

THINGS

I LOVE

What is a stylist really and truly?

A SHOPPER?

A BOSSY BOOTS?

AN ASSEMBLER?

A STRATEGIST WITH PART-PSYCHIC ABILITIES?

A COURIER WITH SLIGHTLY SMARTER CLOTHES ON?

A CAN-DO-ER?

All of these and more.

WHILE EVERY DAY AS A STYLIST THROWS YOU A MAGIC HAND AS WELL AS A CURVEBALL, THERE'S ONE CERTAINTY — WE CHASE, AND HAVE AN INGRAINED RESPECT AND LOVE OF, THINGS. SO HERE, IN NO PARTICULAR ORDER, ARE (SOME) OF THE THINGS I TRULY LOVE (TRUST ME, I COULD DO A WHOLE BOOK ON THIS TOPIC!) I HAVE A PENCHANT FOR PAIRINGS AND HAVE PLACED THESE THINGS TO BE READ AS A SET.

* NOTE: SOME OF THE PAGES ARE PULLOUT-ABLE, IF YOU FANCY. I KNOW, I KNOW, SO KIND. FRAME THEM ON YOUR PIN-BOARD OR GRAB A SINGLE-HOLE PUNCH FOR A TOP CORNER AND, HEY PRESTO — INSTANT GIFT TAG! MY PLEASURE...

NANNA FLOWERS.

Summer – request gardenias and crabapples.

Autumn – seek parrot tulips and poppies.

Winter – try velvety little sweet peas in any colour.

Spring – well, spring is ranunculus time!

HOMES WITH HEART AND…

NOTES WITH MEANING.

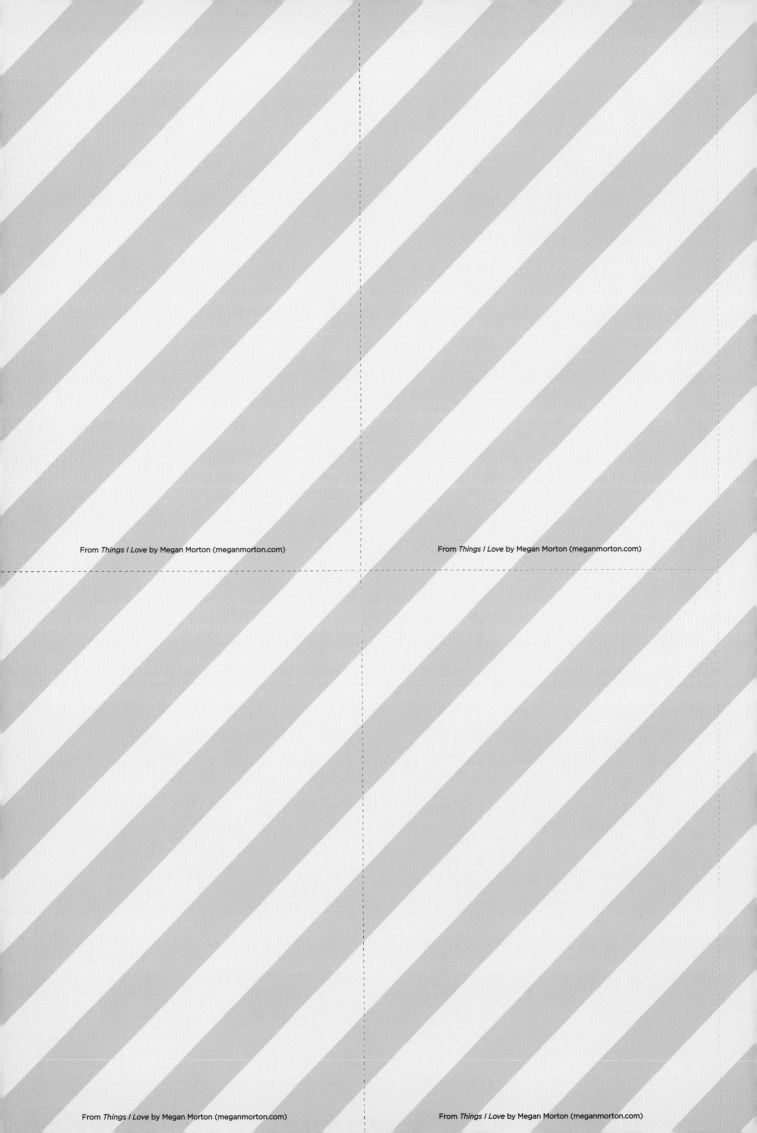

From *Things I Love* by Megan Morton (meganmorton.com)

From *Things I Love* by Megan Morton (meganmorton.com)

From *Things I Love* by Megan Morton (meganmorton.com)

From *Things I Love* by Megan Morton (meganmorton.com)

CLEAN SLATES AND . . .

RULES TO BREAK

- BLUE AND GREEN SHOULD BE WITHOUT A COLOUR BETWEEN.

- YOU DON'T HAVE TO BE AN 'ODD' OR AN 'EVEN' PERSON.

- KITCHENS SHOULD MIMIC A TRIANGLE.

- UTILITY ROOMS SHOULD BE CHEAP AND CHEERFUL.

- PEOPLE MAKE THE CEILING, WALLS AND FLOORS DIFFERENT COLOURS – BUT WHO WANTS TO LIVE WITH GIANT STRIPES?

AUTUMNAL SCRUNCHING.

EDIBLE NAPKIN RINGS.

POST CARD

From *Things I Love* by Megan Morton (meganmorton.com)

POST CARD

From *Things I Love* by Megan Morton (meganmorton.com)

POST CARD

From *Things I Love* by Megan Morton (meganmorton.com)

POST CARD

From *Things I Love* by Megan Morton (meganmorton.com)

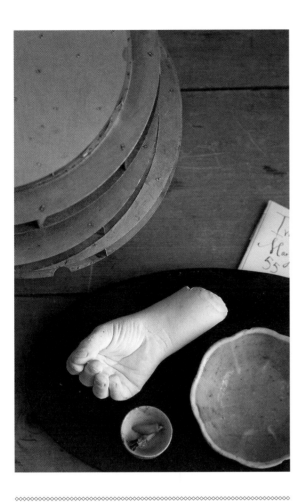

ACT WITH OPEN HEART AND HAND.

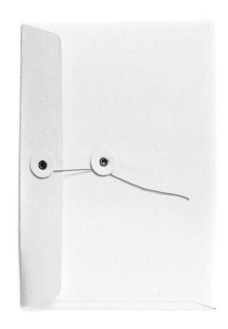

HAIL SNAIL MAIL.

PLAY AT FAIRGROUNDS.

TONAL TABLEAUX.

I
LIKE YOU
LIKE

LIKES

From *Things I Love* by Megan Morton (meganmorton.com)

I
LIKE YOU
LIKE

LIKES

From *Things I Love* by Megan Morton (meganmorton.com)

I
LIKE YOU
LIKE

LIKES

From *Things I Love* by Megan Morton (meganmorton.com)

I
LIKE YOU
LIKE

LIKES

From *Things I Love* by Megan Morton (meganmorton.com)

QUEENSLAND'S NORTH AND…

FRANCE'S SOUTH.

DOMESTIC…

BLISS.

To:

From:

To:

From:

To:

From:

To:

From:

PINWHEELS ON PEGBOARDS.

ORANGE FOR EFFICIENCY.

SINGLES.

PAIRS.

From *Things I Love* by Megan Morton (meganmorton.com)
From *Things I Love* by Megan Morton (meganmorton.com)

From *Things I Love* by Megan Morton (meganmorton.com)
From *Things I Love* by Megan Morton (meganmorton.com)

FIND SOMETHING FABULOUS TO COLLECT…

LIKE A MAGAZINE THAT SENDS SUBSCRIBERS' COPIES
WITHOUT COVER LINES!

AUSTRALIAS.

DAY SPAS.

I

{ .... }

You

You're

{ .... }

You're

{ .... }

I

{ .... }

You

YOU.

GET YOUR MAGPIE ON.

ACT LIKE IT'S V-DAY EVERY DAY.

THE WRITTEN WORD RULES.

BLUE AND ITS SUPERPOWERS.

MEN'S COLLARS. THEY JUST SMELL GOOD.

INEXPLICABLE PURCHASES.

BLUE TRUMPET BY DAVID BAND, ARTIST, RIP.

POST CARD ►

FOR CORRESPONDENCE

FOR ADDRESS ONLY

STAMP
HERE

●

From *Things I Love* by Megan Morton (meganmorton.com)

POST CARD ►

FOR CORRESPONDENCE

FOR ADDRESS ONLY

STAMP
HERE

●

From *Things I Love* by Megan Morton (meganmorton.com)

POST CARD ►

FOR CORRESPONDENCE

FOR ADDRESS ONLY

STAMP
HERE

●

From *Things I Love* by Megan Morton (meganmorton.com)

POST CARD ►

FOR CORRESPONDENCE

FOR ADDRESS ONLY

STAMP
HERE

●

From *Things I Love* by Megan Morton (meganmorton.com)

OBJETS TROUVÉS.

GOLD-STAR WRAPPING.

CANDLELIGHT.

LOTS OF LUCK.

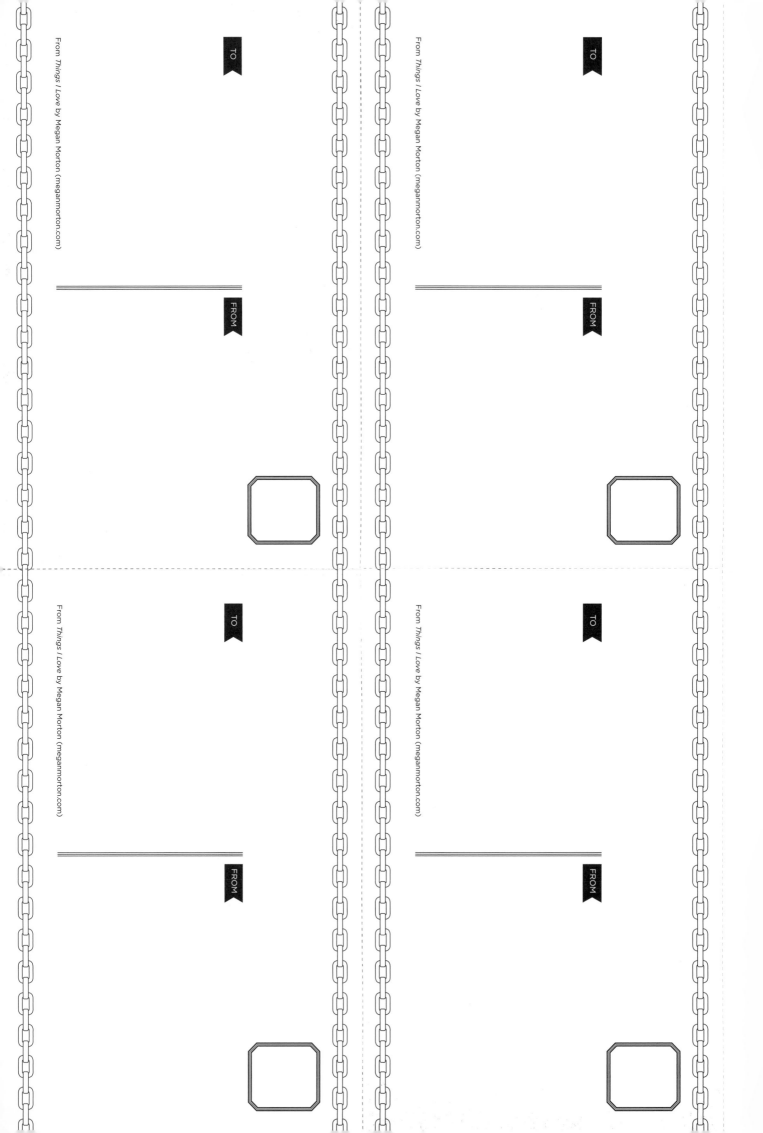

TO

FROM

From *Things I Love* by Megan Morton (meganmorton.com)

TO

FROM

From *Things I Love* by Megan Morton (meganmorton.com)

TO

FROM

From *Things I Love* by Megan Morton (meganmorton.com)

TO

FROM

From *Things I Love* by Megan Morton (meganmorton.com)

PAT & STICK'S ICE-CREAM SANDWICHES AND…

DOGS THAT CHASE STICKS.

THINGS THAT AREN'T NEEDED ANY MORE
BUT STILL MATTER.

I don't know about you, but I suspect that in ten years' time we'll all be in shock that we 'lost' some really lovely things. Things that aren't needed so much any more are my favourite things to collect and enjoy. Try your luck with Polaroid film, packets of HB pencils with handsome wooden barrels, public-transport ticket machines, hats worn by gracious lift operators in swish hotels, compacts made without a hint of plastic, silver napkin rings with monograms, doorbells with sweet chimes.

home ♥ love

From *Things I Love* by Megan Morton (meganmorton.com)

home ♥ love

From *Things I Love* by Megan Morton (meganmorton.com)

home ♥ love

From *Things I Love* by Megan Morton (meganmorton.com)

home ♥ love

From *Things I Love* by Megan Morton (meganmorton.com)

BRAVERY.

BRAVE
DECORATING
MOVES

⭐ **MAKING YOUR HALLWAY DARK NOT LIGHT.**

⭐ **USING DARKS WHERE YOU NATURALLY
   WOULD USE WHITE.**

⭐ **SINGLING OUT ONE COLOUR TO
   LOVE THROUGHOUT.**

⭐ **ZIGGING WHEN OTHERS THOUGHT
   YOU WOULD ZAG.**

LENDING YOUR BOOKS IS GOOD KARMA.

AS IS BUYING UP ON BOOKS.

STAMP
HERE

From *Things I Love* by Megan Morton (meganmorton.com)

STAMP
HERE

From *Things I Love* by Megan Morton (meganmorton.com)

STAMP
HERE

From *Things I Love* by Megan Morton (meganmorton.com)

STAMP
HERE

From *Things I Love* by Megan Morton (meganmorton.com)

BLUE LOVES WHITE.

FLOWER PORTRAITS.

POSTCARDS AND ...

HANDWRITTEN MESSAGES.

To:

From:

To:

From:

To:

From:

To:

From:

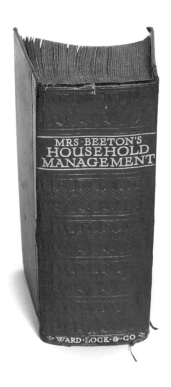

HAIR OF THE DOG.

SAGE ADVICE.

AGEING GRACEFULLY.

LUCI EVERETT'S GARDEN STUDY.

From *Things I Love* by Megan Morton (meganmorton.com)

From *Things I Love* by Megan Morton (meganmorton.com)

ACCESSORISING LIKE YOU'RE…

GOING SOMEWHERE GLAMOROUS.

VINNIES.ORG.AU

SALVOS.ORG.AU

MISSIONAUSTRALIA.COM.AU

GIVE GENEROUSLY. ALWAYS.

EDIT'S SILK SCARVES.

I pledge to support

{ .... }

charity name

in celebration of

{ .... }

recipient's name

for your

{ .... }

insert occasion

THE WONDERFUL
WORLD OF READER'S
DIGEST MUSIC

Bolero

PEOPLE

I LOVE

There are some things some people do better than others – skimming rocks, blowing bubbles, peeling apples, doing embroidery, speaking French or cooking soufflés. Any good stylist is never a sole force, no matter how big they might think themselves. We're more a sum of parts. What we do best is work with other people who are really good at their thing and deliver a result that works for everybody.

My work roster is split over many disciplines – lucky me! One day I might be collaborating with a paper artist, the next a set designer or a specialist merchant or a metalworker. I wanted to share with you the talents and passions of these people. Some work behind the scenes while others are the spokespeople for their craft. Some are super superstars while others are unsung heroes. Some are the reason I wanted to be a stylist in the first place. They're all beyond talented. They're *all* amazing! Facebook should have a 'Love' button for this lot. ▲

HOLLY HIPWELL

The Flower Whisperer

Reading the answers from The Flower Drum's Holly Hipwell (yes, it's her real name!) is as good as having a coffee with her (warning, she only drinks soy). Everything you need to know is here and everything she says is true. Her I-can't-eat-my-dinner-at-night-because-I-love-peonies-so-much world is real. And contagious. I opened my school with her flower bomb class and we nearly broke the internet with the carnation-love picture-sharing. ▲

What's your middle name?
Lara Le Hunte.

Who were you before The Flower Drum?
I once was Holly Hipwell the Helicopter Hostess.

What's the best thing about not being trained as a florist?
Learning how not to do things wrong and creating out of curiosity instead of procedure.

What's your best floral moment so far?
Creating the wedding bouquet for one of my best friends on her wedding day then watching her walk down the aisle to become Mrs Rose! Oh, and another time I was paid to write swear words with flowers . . .

If I were a flower, I'd be . . .
One that drops its petals a lot.

If you had to marry a rose grower or a butcher, which would you choose?
A butcher. If I had to pick between a steak and a rose . . .

Home is . . .
Where you and your things belong. Actually, I'm about to move into my DIY dream home with candy-stripe flooring!

What's your favourite object at home?
I inherited from my mother a penchant for buying items that won't fit in the car/aeroplane/boat but insisting on taking these finds home. They're my favourites.

Swan dive or cannonball?
People often ask me if I can swim – I think it's because I'm pale. Definitely cannonball.

Tell us one thing *no one* knows about you
I have a major complex about saying people's names out loud.

Are all flowers nice?
The sweeter the smell of a rose, the more thorns it has to stab you with.

LYDIA PEARSON

The Trailblazers

Years back, I styled for the shoot of Lydia Pearson's family home in Queensland. It was, of course, beautiful, and it was a breakthrough story for me early in my career. This was nothing to do with me and all to do with Lydia's raspberry-striped living-room ceiling. Genius! It wasn't a styled shot by any means, but people still talk about it to this day. It's the one shot people stop at when they view my portfolio. I will be forever grateful. Lydia is one half of fashion house Easton Pearson's design partnership (Pamela Easton is the other). In 2009, Brisbane's GOMA (Gallery of Modern Art) held an exhibition of Easton Pearson's work, in celebration of the company's twentieth anniversary. You should've seen it. No words. ▲

What went through your mind when you walked into your show at GOMA?
It was the pineapples arranged over the pineapple wallpaper that took my breath away. Pineapples have been our icon for so very long, and they are a symbol of hospitality and welcome. They set just the right mood of opulence and irreverence (especially because it was Queensland) that seemed to epitomise the spirit of our exhibition. And then the women, so many decked out in our clothes, and frequently matching one of the exhibition mannequins!

Our work is all about . . .
Detail, colour and ornamentation of form.

What does a working day look like for you?
An early start; many, many cups of jasmine tea; sitting with Pam in the office to do admin and planning, then potentially working together on either fabrication, print design, shapes for the collection or fitting patterns; at least one quick dive down to the Flamingo café, as much for the repartee and fresh air as the need for actual sustenance; multiple conversations with our team, always with something to laugh about and occasional lockjaw or tears; if we're lucky, a 6 p.m. finish or if on deadline, closer to 9 or 10 p.m.

Two skills you'll put to use this week:
▸ **Ingenuity.**
▸ **Creativity.**

If I were a flower, I'd be . . .
An extravagance of jasmine and antigonon, with white peonies and cunjevoi leaves.

What's your favourite colour combination?
We coloured our new rugs today, and we seem to be rather fond of a deep peacock mixed with ginger browns and sulfur-yellow highlights.

I know it's daggy but I love . . .
Playing Scrabble with endless cups of tea.

What's the most played song or set on your iPod?
Well, I don't have an iPod with music on, but I do have a current obsession with Nadéah from Nouvelle Vague, singing 'Master and Servant' and playing the melodica. Of course, as she's most extremely decorative, it's best to watch on YouTube!

My favourite colour is . . .
In constant flux.

I like to use it . . .
Extravagantly.

What's your favourite room in the house and why?
Our bedroom. It's high among the trees, sitting near the sky, with the patterns of clouds in the morning, and the moon and stars at night.

What makes a house special?
When it truly reflects the life and loves of its owner(s), and is accommodating of the idiosyncrasies of their life(lives); when the decor has evolved with careful regard to an individual aesthetic and little regard to current decorating fads.

What's your favourite hotel?
For work, Le Pavillon de la Reine in Paris – I can't imagine spending Paris Fashion Week anywhere else. For holidays, a campervan is my ideal.

In three words my living room is . . .
Celestial, generous, artisanal.

My favourite season is . . .
Winter so we can have a fire, spring because we can open the big windows, summer so I can lie in bed and watch the sun come up, autumn because I can cook . . .

I'd spend my last decorative dollar on . . .
Really good furniture polish so I could look after what I already have, or, if it were a big last dollar, a copper-panelled front door. Ours was abandoned in that inevitable cost-cutting at the end of a project.

List some titles from your reading stack
▸ **_Voltaire in Love_ by Nancy Mitford**

If I weren't me, I'd be . . .
An astronomer with a fantastic memory.

My favourite charity is . . .
The Indigenous Literacy Foundation, equal with the Fred Hollows Foundation.

Tell me a thing, or some things, I didn't know about you.
I love swing dancing (that's enthusiasm, not ability).

Who's your favourite astrologer?
Mystic Meg.

BRONWYN RIEDEL

The Colour Scientist

It's a mad process to witness: give Bronwyn a hair from your labrador, or a celery stick, and watch her sprinkle pigments into a bowl until the colour is exactly right and then pour finished paint into a tin with a special coded ID. We half-jokingly call her Rainman! It won't just be right to the eye, but scientifically right. She knows that colour is a science and she can tell you exactly which colours are friends of which others. She divides her time between her home in Perth, where Bauwerk has a store, their colour studio in Dubai and her Rittergut (knight's manor) in the former East Germany, which is surrounded by elderberry, wildflowers, herbs, yarrow and cow parsley. This 21-room neoclassical house that was once baroque has Europe's oldest plane tree in the front yard! If you ever get the chance to meet Bronwyn in Bauwerk's Perth store, make sure you take note of what she's wearing, for no other reason than that it will be the most perfect tonal combination ever. I still remember the softest peach coral colliding with donkey-bottom grey at our first meeting. Total perfection! ▲

My work is all about . . .
Lots of different things, mostly growth and all that entails, lots of organising and planning – I always seem to have a project going on, and I go from one thing to the next depending on where I am. In Saudi Arabia I spend a lot of time on marketing our new products, in Australia I get to have a lot of fun developing new colours.

What gets you up in the morning?
Endless things to do, which I start thinking about as soon as I wake up, and the thought of breakfast and coffee with friends.

If I were a flower, I'd be . . .
A bunch of wild meadow flowers in lots of different colours and shapes, nothing ordered or perfect, in a big vase.

I know it's daggy but I love . . .
Trash TV, especially anything about decorating.

My favourite colour is . . .
Anything moody and complex.

I like to use it . . .
In fabrics and paints.

Home is . . .
Everything.

My dream holiday goes something like this:
Arrive, get a car, drive wherever my eye takes me, have no plans, explore, wander, eat local fantastic fresh real food, spend lots of time talking, rediscovering and dreaming with my husband, Andreas.

Describe your design process.
Immersion in anything beautiful, letting ideas and inspiration come by sitting down somewhere alone, usually a café, and then spilling it all out, or walking and letting designs or ideas come into my mind. I can usually see everything I do first as a picture or feeling in my head.

What does a working day look like for you?
From fantastically inspiring and fun to hard and frustrating.

What's the best thing to eat in Fremantle?
Abhi's Bread sunflower sesame loaf with fresh avocado.

List some titles from your reading stack.
‣ *Plenty* by Yotam Ottolenghi (cookbook)
‣ *Girl by Sea* by Penelope Green
‣ *Dumbo Feather* magazine

The good life is . . .
The life you have with all the people you love.

Tell me a thing, or some things, I didn't know about you.
I'm scared of failure, I'm a besotted mother, I used to sing in a reggae band, I grew up on a farm in the Strathbogie Ranges.

What are your favourite words in German and Arabic?
In German it's *schön*, which means lovely, beautiful, good, etc. I completely overuse it, which Germans think is very funny, as they're not that exuberant. My favourite Arabic word is *alhamdulillah*, which literally means 'thanks be to God' but is used widely to say you're in good health. The feeling you get from the word is that you're held by something bigger than yourself.

What would your self-portrait look like?
I'd draw myself reclining on a chaise longue, curves and all.

RUSSELL PINCH

The Furniture Designer

Anyone who's ever bought a lounge can attest to the fact that the difference really is in the details. Russell Pinch is an insightful man who happens to design, in my opinion, the perfect lounge: the feet, the seat depth, the arm width, everything about his Claude lounge is perfect for an informal living space. Not supermodel perfect, more like Sophie Dahl perfect. For me, Pinch's furniture is all about restraint but never skimping. It feels full, but not like you're in over your head, just nicely head-above-the-waterline full. This is deliberate, so you can add bits that make it yours. Nice. It's like you're in collaboration with him without even knowing it.▲

Describe the Pinch design philosophy in three words.
Engaging, crafted, integrity.

If I were a fashion designer I'd be . . .
Elie Saab.

If you could design anything in the world, what would it be?
A cliff-edge hut with a hell of a view. I'd design the exterior, the interior and everything in it.

Who's on your blog roll?
What's a blog?

My favourite flower, colour and animal are . . .
Poppies, yellow, hares (alive), crabs (dead).

What's the best thing you did this year?
Spend the first night in a house we've been building for seven years.

Who or what inspires you?
Oona.

Are you a water or meadows person?
Meadows.

Where's your happy place?
Charmeneuil, on the west coast of France.

What's your favourite type of client?
One who trusts us and is ambitious, with a sparkle in their eye.

What are you reading right now?
Mostly *Charlie and Lola*, *Miffy* and Roald Dahl, but when I get to choose, *The Guardian*.

What does a working day look like for you?
Be woken early by small people, take Ada to school, cycle to work, work (making models, meeting clients, workshop visits), home for playtime with the kids, radio comedy and a long cook-up, dinner, plenty of wine, an open fire at any opportunity, bed.

My dream holiday goes something like this:
Somewhere with a view, somewhere remote but with good access to fantastic seafood, bike rides, days outside, all afternoon spent planning the barbecue dinner, eating outside with the sun going down.

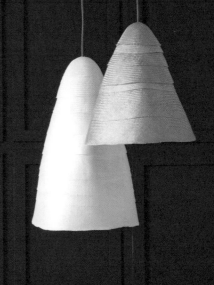

SASHA TITCHKOSKY & RUSSEL KOSKELA

The Pioneers

Aeons ago I visited my friends at their showroom. They had just started Koskela as a business and had given me a book to read: *New Alchemists* by Irish philosopher Charles Handy, all about modern thinkers in creative business. What I read made me positively dizzy. They themselves have become an extraordinary success story, much like those profiled in Handy's book. Do you know how hard it is to manufacture and market in Australia? Oh, Koskela, we thank you for trying so hard and doing it so well. Made in Australia – totally – their products are our flag-flyers for what's good, what's wholesome and what's truly Australian, with zero cringe factor. Get a piece of the Koskela pie at their new showroom in Sydney, or rent their charming weekender, Dickebusch (the name is a long, long story!). ▲

Our work is all about . . .
ST: **Designing great pieces that stand the test of time and that might bring a smile to your face every time you use them. We also get a kick out of working with Australian manufacturers – partly to prove wrong all those people who told us to go to China when we first started.**

What gets you up in the morning?
RK: **I love our company. I love the thrill of coming up with an idea and then working with people whose skill I admire to turn those ideas into a reality.**
ST: **I think it's pretty hard to beat seeing an idea actually come to fruition.**

If I were a flower, I'd be . . .
RK: **Well, it would have to be something a bit, you know, macho. No posy here! Maybe a big old man banksia.**
ST: **Maybe something like a japonica (ornamental quince), nice but with the odd prickle.**

I know it's daggy but I love . . .
RK: **Golf – is that daggy? Or fishing?**
ST: **I love golf too.**

My favourite colour is . . .
RK: **Fluoro red and rust at the moment – in combination with natural textures and materials.**
ST: **I'm going through a small crush on fluoro colours at the moment. Okay, it's quite a big crush, actually. I like them everywhere in small doses – there's something so uplifting about them.**

Where do you go for inspiration?
RK: **I really love going to factories. I get a lot of ideas from looking at manufacturing processes and materials. I also love going to the big wide-open spaces in the bush.**
ST: **I do love *Spanish Architectural Digest* and also *Uppercase* magazines.**

What's your best décor or design advice?
RK: **Follow your heart, trust your judgement, do it with joy.**
ST: **Just make it real and throw out the rule book. It's your home – don't worry what it *should* be like, let it be what you like.**

Home is . . .
RK: **Somewhere that reflects you, how you live, what's special to you, memories of years gone by. I don't think it should ever be a prescriptive, templated formula.**
ST: **Somewhere you can feel a sense of peace and somewhere you feel you belong.**

My dream holiday goes something like this:
RK: **Something that has the following ingredients: action, experience, design, local handicraft and then relaxation.**
ST: **A lot like Russel's, really, except maybe with a massage thrown in here and there.**

I'd spend my last decorative dollar on . . .
RK: **A Mabel Juli canvas from Warmun in the East Kimberley.**
ST: **I'd probably say some art. I'm just a little bit in love with Joseph McGlennon's photography – his Kangaroo series in particular – but I could also just spend it on some nice old photograph or artwork as well.**

If I weren't me, I'd be a . . .
RK: **Professional golfer.**
ST: **I don't know. I always wanted to be a doctor and work in disadvantaged communities.**

Who's on your blog roll?
RK: **trendland.net, designboom.com, applegreenapple.tumblr.com.**

The good life is . . .
RK: **Hanging out at Patonga with my two boys and missus – enjoying a bit of fishing, swimming, beach barbecues. It doesn't get much better than that.**
ST: **Cooking, eating and drinking with friends at a campfire on Patonga beach.**

Tell me a thing, or some things,
I didn't know about you.
ST: **My middle name is Anna, and it's also the middle name of one of my sisters as well as my mother's first name!**

TSÉ & TSÉ ASSOCIÉS

The Charmers

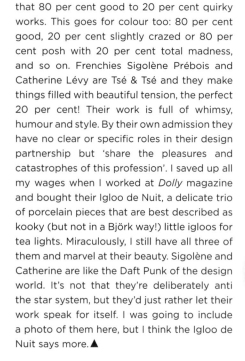

I'm of the opinion (for my own house anyway) that 80 per cent good to 20 per cent quirky works. This goes for colour too: 80 per cent good, 20 per cent slightly crazed or 80 per cent posh with 20 per cent total madness, and so on. Frenchies Sigolène Prébois and Catherine Lévy are Tsé & Tsé and they make things filled with beautiful tension, the perfect 20 per cent! Their work is full of whimsy, humour and style. By their own admission they have no clear or specific roles in their design partnership but 'share the pleasures and catastrophes of this profession'. I saved up all my wages when I worked at *Dolly* magazine and bought their Igloo de Nuit, a delicate trio of porcelain pieces that are best described as kooky (but not in a Björk way!) little igloos for tea lights. Miraculously, I still have all three of them and marvel at their beauty. Sigolène and Catherine are like the Daft Punk of the design world. It's not that they're deliberately anti the star system, but they'd just rather let their work speak for itself. I was going to include a photo of them here, but I think the Igloo de Nuit says more. ▲

What does a working day look like for you?
SP & CL: Meeting with each other in our office, going for lunch, and spending the afternoon dealing with many different things, very randomly.

Our work is all about …
SP & CL: Having fun, enjoying ourselves, making people smile.

If I were a flower, I'd be …
SP: I'm not a flower.
CL: A pumpkin flower.

My favourite colour is …
SP & CL: Rainbow.

I like to use …
SP & CL: Bikes, hammers, lipstick, a sharp knife and all our products.

Where do you go for inspiration?
SP & CL: To all kinds of markets and flea markets, in Paris, out of Paris, all over the world.

My dream holiday goes something like this:
SP: Walk barefoot on warm tiles.
CL: Travel through Turkey, Iran and Pakistan to India.

Describe your design process.
SP & CL: We design something when we need or want it for ourselves.

What's the best thing to eat in Paris?
SP & CL: Cheese, oysters, chestnut bread, buckwheat bread, *choux à la crème*.

List some titles from your reading stack.
SP: *Les Choses (Things)* by Georges Perec.
CL: I'm dreaming of rereading Jack London.

The good life is …
SP & CL: Filled with small everyday pleasures.

The most common cliché about the French is …
SP & CL: That they're noisy and rude, but it's not a cliché!

Tell me a thing, or some things, I didn't know about you.
SP & CL: We met when we were sixteen and we were trying to be punk.

Anything else you'd like to share?
SP & CL: We like to share things! That's why we can work together.

NADINE INGRAM

The Baker

Nadine Ingram treats her baking duties as seriously as an artist takes to their canvas: she's diligent, extreme and precise. She makes macaroons, among other things, and this is how we met – I wanted to send something to clients when we wrapped up their job that wasn't a bunch of flowers or a potted orchid. So we sent boxes of Nadine's macaroons made from the fluff of champagne. We had to stop sending them because before too long I was ordering one for us at the office for every box we sent out. To know Nadine is to eat at her café/bakery called Flour and Stone (named in honour of her daughters, Poppy and Ruby). You might not meet her in person, but you will meet her in spirit, in the food and atmosphere she's provided. ▲

My work is all about . . .
The sweetness of life.

What gets you up in the morning?
Ambition.

If I were a flower, I'd be . . .
A stem of lilac hanging over an English lane.

My favourite colour is . . .
Green in all its shades.

I like to use it . . .
To colour my pistachio macaroons.

I know it's daggy but I love . . .
Lionel Richie.

My favourite macaroon flavour is . . .
Hazelnut and coffee.

What's your favourite room in the house and why?
My bedroom because of the peace and the pillowcases by Castle.

My living room is . . .
Dark and moody.

What makes a house special?
Art, books and colour.

My dream holiday goes something like this:
A bakery/patisserie crawl of Europe with a side trip to Tartine in San Francisco.

What does a working day look like for you?
Baking a shop full of goodness before the sun comes up. The rest of my day can be varied: helping to ice or roll cookies, training staff or meeting with brides to discuss their wedding cake. Every day is different and this is what I love most about running my own business. I try to leave the shop around 2.30 so I can collect my two daughters from school.

I'd spend my last decorative dollar on . . .
Pieces by Melissa Egan or Kendal Murray.

List some titles from your reading stack.
▸ *Breakfast, Lunch, Tea: Rose Bakery* by Rose Carrarini (I love Rose's ethos on food)
▸ *10 Mindful Minutes* by Goldie Hawn
▸ *Florence Broadhurst: Her Secret & Extraordinary Lives* by Helen O'Neill

My favourite charity is . . .
Oxfam.

My favourite animal is . . .
A happy free-range chicken.

The good life is . . .
When you live surrounded by creativity, art and love, but most of all not letting it pass you by.

Tell me a thing, or some things, I didn't know about you.
When I was a little girl I wanted to be an interior designer. My mum gave me a budget to decorate our living room and I spent it on papasans and Ken Done fabric. It was so 1980s.

RACHEL CASTLE

The Sunshine

It's true. She *is* sunshine. Her embroidered artwork ('It's Christmas Eve' by the Pogues, 'Hallelujah', 'Death of a Disco Dancer') shows her vintage, but her screen-printing shows her complete love of colour and its mood-changing capabilities. She reluctantly calls it art, but it so is – just ask the thousands of people around the world who send her pictures of their invigorated mantelpieces or their babies asleep on her fluoro-spot pillowcases. As soon as her children leave for school, the house turns into a full-service print and stitching studio. Her fingers are always sore, but her head keeps inventing new things for them to keep up with. It's truly a family affair – her mum, Jillian, is her standby stitcher, her daughter Cleo gives her strong opinion about what she deems is hot or not, and her son Lucky gives – just by being himself – hilariously good inspiration, hence the 'I Love Homework' artwork. Her husband, Daren, just thinks she's the cleverest thing out – he makes her chunky heart shapes out of wood off-cuts. ▲

My work is all about …
It's a spot thing.
It's a love of high-voltage colour and a song to sing loudly. It's only ever about love.

My favourite colour is …
Yellow.

I like to use it …
Everywhere.

What makes a house special?
Art and music, equally.

My dream holiday goes something like this:
Happy children, happy husband, swimming, books, cards, sangria, staying out too late, eating all day long, waking up and doing it all over again.

What gets you up in the morning?
Early morning yoga or before-school band practice, but mostly my noisy, can't-lie-still husband.

If I were a flower, I'd be …
A colourful bunch that would sit perfectly well in a kitchen corner.

What's your favourite colour combination?
Can I have two please? Bronze and lilac. Gold and pink.

I know it's daggy but I love …
Fleetwood Mac and party pies

My lounge at home is …
Ten-year-old twin Conran sofas. They're like beds – I can't sit on either of them without falling asleep instantly.

In three words my living room is …
Full of stuff.

My favourite season is …
Summer, summer, summer and summer.

I'd spend my last decorative dollar on …
Tinsel.

My favourite charity is …
Lou's Place, a women's day refuge in Kings Cross where I teach sewing on Wednesday mornings.

What does a working day look like for you?
Hectic. Once the children have left I get straight to work. I like to have a few things on the go at once, so I might take the printing table out and start to ink up an order. While the first couple of prints are drying I'll do paperwork – yuck! – and then settle down to some serious felt cutting. Then I sit down to sew. When the children come home, I taxi them around to all their bits and bobs, and then from eight to eleven I work again – same routine without the printing; it's too dark by then.

What's the most played song or set on your iPod?
I'm in a choir, which I love, so it's usually a voice part of something that I need to learn in detail. It's normally in another language, often about God. I love the requiems the best – very dark and dramatic.

Two skills I'll put to use this week:
▸ Sweeping. I have to sweep the workroom floor habitually. It's covered in felt and cotton and paper, which sticks to my shoes in big balls and which I then walk through the house. There's cotton/fabric/felt debris in every single room of our house. I even sometimes find it in the garden. My lovely next-door neighbour and I were very excited to discover a nest in her front tree made by a bird using some fluoro-orange and bright-blue cotton, which could only have come from one place.
▸ Saying no to all the 'extracurriculars' that throw everything off balance.

List some titles from your reading stack.
Any and all of the magazines, plus *Wolf Hall* by Hilary Mantel – it's big, stunning and complicated. It's been halfway around the world and I still haven't finished it – the front cover has fallen off.

Tell me a thing, or some things, I didn't know about you.
My husband and I met and married within six weeks exactly. My mother is better at sewing than I am. My husband couldn't cut a felt spot to save himself.

LISA COOPER
The Artist

It was in Lisa's dreamy apartment that I first saw canvas drop sheets used successfully as curtains. They looked so good I wanted to punch her. She'd just painted the apartment and the sheet had that perfect measure of accidental white-paint staining without looking feral. Come to think of it, just about everything Lisa and her partner, Eliza, do is beautiful. Special. Considered. Art informs their every move, and their quality of life is enhanced by the sun that fills their north-facing 1920s apartment through its zigzag windows. Everyone who gets their photo taken in this special window area looks more pleased with themselves than they deserve to. It's a special apartment, too. The new paint clings to the super-old plaster of the walls, which has a pleasing sense of coldness that's only noticeable on sunny Sydney days. Or maybe it's Eliza's iced tea and gracious hospitality. Some ladies know how to live and these two do it really, really well. ▲

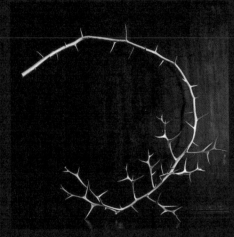

My work is all about …
**Imaging internal
states. Projecting
emotion.
Metaphoring
experience.**

What gets you up
in the morning?
Love and coffee.

If I were a flower,
I'd be a …
**Blown red garden
rose (held by Saint
Thérèse of Lisieux).**

I know it's daggy
but I love …
**The aesthetics of
Catholicism and
A Current Affair –
I can't believe the
stories it covers, like
phenomenal Diet
Coke addicts.**

My favourite
colour is …
Gold.

I like to use it …
**On my nails,
paintings, sculpture,
as leaf, as a tooth in my
mouth, in powder form
on my cheekbones.**

Where do you go
for inspiration?
**To the past and
New York.**

What's your best décor
or design advice?
**Linens should
be white.**

My dream holiday
goes something like this:
**Clear blue waters,
personal chef,
pear cider, books.**

Describe your
design process.
**Intuitive,
compositional,
layered (no drawings).**

What does a working
day look like for you?
**Walk – Cee Lo Green,
Eminem and the like;
a.m. – make whatever
needs making
(video, painting,
sculpture, flowers);
p.m. – emails,
grant applications,
correspondence,
meetings.**

What's the best thing
to eat in Sydney?
**Anything Kylie Kwong
sees fit to dish up.**

I'd spend my last
decorative dollar on …
Really long matches.

If I weren't me,
I'd be a …
Philosopher or mum.

List some titles from
your reading stack.
▸ *Just Kids* by
   Patti Smith
▸ *The Infinity
   Machine: Mike
   Parr's Performance
   Art 1971–2005*
   by Edward Scheer
▸ *Art and Fear*
   by Paul Virilio

The good life is …
Green and free.

Tell me a thing,
or some things,
I didn't know about you.
**One of my great-
grandfathers was
the quickest boner
(butcher) in New South
Wales; another was
nearly a priest (before
he fell in love).**

What would
a self-portrait of you
look like?
**gold
tears
scent
love**

JULIE PATERSON

The Fabric Artist

When Julie saw the Australian bush for the first time, she had her true aha moment. With a painting studio and home in the Blue Mountains, she observes scrub, wildlife and often-harsh Australia at its most beautiful. Her paintings, fabrics and rugs deal with water (and lack of it), birds, mountains and sheds. Her day job is as the boss lady at Cloth, her fabric company, but she always has her eye on the prize – a weekend's painting in her Mountains studio. From her own observation, she's decided we should live with furniture that's semi-distressed and aged, as it's 'totally flattering'. Too true! ▲

If I were a flower, I'd be . . .
A thicket of kangaroo paw or maybe a small but intensely coloured native iris.

I know it's daggy but I love . . .
Sending postcards to my mum and dad.

Seaside or meadows? Sweet or savoury? Bubbles in wine?
The ocean, the mountains, cheese and biscuits, a cup of strong tea, gin and tonic, tomatoes on toast.

My favourite colour is . . .
Old lady red, of course.

I like to use it . . .
As a singlet poking out under a grey T-shirt or as the bottom sheet on my bed or as a pair of boots, but never as lipstick or curtains.

What's your best décor or design advice?
Don't take it too seriously. A cushion is just a cushion, after all.

Describe your design process.
I draw, I sketch, I collect things, I hang out in my studio and make stuff, I think about what I've made and talk to people about it until gradually whatever it is comes into being.

What does a working day look like for you?
Well, an ideal day would be one where, after the cup of tea in bed, I'd walk to the studio for a few hours and carry on making things that I'd been making the day before. Then I'd cycle to my shop in Surry Hills and talk to my team about Important Stuff for a few hours. Then I'd cycle back home, go for a swim then maybe back to the studio for a bit more tinkering until the light fades. Sometimes these ideal days happen, sometimes they don't.

I'd spend my last decorative dollar on . . .
A new small piece of art or a second-hand chair.

If I weren't me, I'd be a . . .
Drummer/backing singer in a girl band that was particularly successful in Japan due to our wacky costumes and offbeat lyrics.

List some titles from your reading stack.
▸ *How the Water Feels to the Fishes* **by Dave Eggers**
▸ *The Gathering* **by Anne Enright**
▸ *Fires* **by Raymond Carver**
▸ *Start Where You Are* **by Pema Chödrön**
▸ *The Bee Hut* **by Dorothy Porter**

The good life is . . .
Reading my way through all those books before I start work.

Tell me a thing, or some things, I didn't know about you.
I don't have a middle name and as a kid I always wanted one. So I decided it would be Elizabeth due to my obsession with imagining the Queen going to the toilet.

KIM HURLEY

The Button Merchant

My work is all about . . .
Creating objects or environments that delight
the viewer in some way, through the use of
beautiful colours, whimsy and nostalgia.

What gets you up in the morning?
My cat.

If I were a flower, I'd be a posy of . . .
Carnations, sweet peas and roses,
all from my grandfather's garden.

I know it's daggy but I love . . .
Real mail, not email.

My favourite colour is . . .
I couldn't possibly choose just one: blush, puce,
pale aqua, rich burgundy, French blues, intense
deep pink, gold, bronze – I could go on. I do
like colour to be a little dirty, not too pure
and clean.

I like to use . . .
My suitcase. I love the sound of the wheels –
it means I'm travelling.

What's your best décor or design advice?
Opposites attract: if you love pale soft colours,
inject a hit of a stronger colour somewhere;
if you love strong colour, incorporate a little
neutral colour – this will make the elements
you love stand out more and provide balance
to the overall look.

Home is . . .
Time at home sometimes feels like a luxury,
so much of my time seems spent elsewhere,
but when the door closes and the world slips
away a little, it's like you decompress –
it's what keeps me sane.

My dream holiday goes something like this:
Paris – apartment in the Marais with friends;
Vienna – Schönbrunn Palace in the snow;
train through the snow-covered alps to Venice –
rent an apartment for three misty, snowy weeks;
Florence; Rome.

What does a working day look like for you?
I start late and finish late – I hate peak-
hour traffic. I'm either working on props for
upcoming window displays, manufacturing
l'uccello products and shipping out orders,
running the shop and looking after customers,
or sourcing materials and stock.

What's the best thing to eat in Melbourne?
The tuna entrée at Svago in Kew.

If I weren't me, I'd be . . .
The girl who rides the white pony at the circus.

List some titles from your reading stack.
▸ *Paper Illusions: The Art of Isabelle de
  Borchgrave* by Barbara & René Stoeltie
▸ *Collected Works* by Rupert Brooke
▸ *Dangerous Liaisons* by Pierre Choderlos
  de Laclos
▸ *Selvedge* magazine

**Tell me a thing, or some things,
I didn't know about you.**
I can't bear raw tomato or The Beatles.

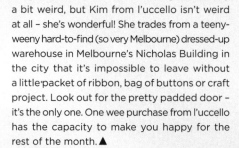

People who deal in the one thing are usually
a bit weird, but Kim from l'uccello isn't weird
at all – she's wonderful! She trades from a teeny-
weeny hard-to-find (so very Melbourne) dressed-up
warehouse in Melbourne's Nicholas Building in
the city that it's impossible to leave without
a little packet of ribbon, bag of buttons or craft
project. Look out for the pretty padded door –
it's the only one. One wee purchase from l'uccello
has the capacity to make you happy for the
rest of the month. ▲

LUCELLO.BLOGSPOT.COM

MATTHEW COLLINS

The Master of Forgotten Crafts

I love Tadelakt, the old-style polished lime plaster wall treatment. Only a handful of people do it in Australia: Matthew is one of them and boy, does he have a beautiful hand? Tadelakt is as much about what you don't put on as what you do. Someone who can perform it is quite a genius, which is why Matthew's work in wallpapers, surfaces or painted finishes has the same breathtaking quality. He can even make bathroom walls take on the appearance of a decadent *hammam* in a Moroccan resort. ▲

My work is all about . . .
Reflections of nature, the passage of time and the patina left in its wake.

What gets you up in the morning?
A boyish love of early starts, getting into the studio with time to have a cup of tea and tidy my space. A tidy studio equals a creative, productive and joy-filled day.

If I were a flower, I'd be . . .
Gorse, spiky and savage, strangely delicate, beautiful at a distance en masse and when lit capable of burning with amazing intensity.

I know it's daggy but I love . . .
Choral music – Poulenc, Fauré and above all Górecki.

Seaside or meadows? Sweet or savoury? Bubbles in wine?
I grew up on a smallholding on the west Wales coast so I've always hankered after a mellifluous blend of beach and meadow. I always go savoury – but you'd better hide the homemade raspberry ice-cream – and I can drink champagne till I'm red in the face.

My favourite colour is . . .
Midnight blue.

I like to use . . .
My ridiculously large brush collection.

Where do you go for inspiration?
Anywhere lichen creeps over branches and rocks.

What's your best décor or design advice?
Either be very specific about what you want or give your designer free rein.

Describe your design process.
I make a list of all the things I love, then try to do something that combines them all, working with plaster and waxes, oils, earths and oxides. I then edit with a savage heart.

What does a working day look like for you?
I'm into the studio at 6.15 a.m., have a tidy, do some paperwork and have some cups of tea, work on samples, go out for meetings on site, then back to the studio to reconcile the day and finish some samples before heading home some time around 5 p.m.

What's the best thing to eat in Melbourne?
The charcuterie plate at Cumulus, veggie balls at Ebi (Japanese fish and chip shop), the sausage pizza at Tabet's Lebanese Bakery on Sydney Road.

If I weren't me, I'd be . . .
An entomologist wearing a pith helmet, deep in the forests of the Amazon collecting new species of butterfly.

List some titles from your reading stack.
▶ *Caught by the River: A Collection of Words on Water* edited by Jeff Barrett, Robin Turner & Andrew Walsh
▶ *The Cloudspotter's Guide* by Gavin Pretor-Pinney
▶ *The Book of Symbols: Reflections on Archetypal Images* by the Archive for Research in Archetypal Symbolism (ARAS)

Tell me a thing, or some things, I didn't know about you.
I started collecting butterflies when I was five years old. I later found out that my great-grandfather was a renowned entomologist whose collection now resides in the Liverpool Natural History Museum . . . Darn!

Anything else you'd like to share?
Nobody really knows what I do, neither my family nor my friends. They all know something of what I do, but if they ever got together to chat, they'd all think they knew someone different. This is mainly because I do something different every week. I make handmade wallpaper and I do murals, Tadelakt, paint finishes, polished plasters and gilding. I also consult on projects as an interior designer and decorator and have had work as an art director on television series. I make surfaces and backdrops for stylists and photographers. I'm an artist. Phew! I used to teach decorative finishes at the weekend as well but that was just getting silly and I let it slip.

ANTONY TODD

The Good Time Guy

I once crashed my car reading a story about Antony Todd at home, sharing his creative pursuits and process. When I got home, everyone was all: 'Are you okay? What happened?' How could I admit that the way Todd used my favourite shade of blue with stone made me run into a pole? His colour control was just the beginning. The story told of one of his low-key dinner gatherings where he leaves little red threads (that double as napkin ties) for guests to tie around their neighbour's wrist as a sign of friendship. The guy has done mega-balls and counts megastars on his client roster, but at the end of the day, he knows how to make everyone – no matter how many people are in the one room – feel special. It comes across through his flowers, his parties, his homes and his products. Although he's made it in New York, this Australian splits his time between the Big Apple and Istanbul. It's this contrast that makes his work so flavoursome. ▲

My work is all about . . .
Creating beauty, be it interiors, for events or entertaining. We've had amazing word-of-mouth referrals. Every small job seemed to pass around the same positive message and it just kept growing little by little.

If I were a flower, I'd be . . .
A large, heavenly, creamy, off-white tree magnolia or gardenia flower.

I know it's daggy but I love . . .
Mmmm, my shower cap and face mask before an important evening event in New York City – it really works!

My favourite colour is . . .
Navy blue.

I like to use it . . .
Mostly in my clothing, occasionally in natural suede on period French dining chairs, once the wood has been stripped down and waxed to natural nude-wood colour.

Where do you go for inspiration?
Being on the road about six months of the year allows so much fulfilling inspiration, so not really one place. The views across to the old city and down the Bosphorus from my home, the call to prayer, the architecture and light of Istanbul – they all inspire me.

What's your best décor or design advice?
Logic when designing and good editing.

My dream holiday goes something like this:
Barefoot, not too many clothes, no phones, good food, booze and lots of laughter.

Describe your design process.
Step one is definitely meeting with the client and seeing the location, understanding their needs, understanding them and what they're looking to achieve. After that the design process begins.

I'd spend my last decorative dollar on . . .
Beautiful textiles or art.

If I weren't me, I'd be . . .
I've never thought of being anybody else.

List some titles from your reading stack.
▸ *The Forty Rules of Love* by Elif Şafak
▸ The *Financial Times* (the state of the world concerns me daily)

The good life is . . .
Time with people I love – my niece, godchildren and friends, my partner and our dog, Tobi.

Tell me a thing, or some things, I didn't know about you.
I'm a home-body who very few people know. I make excellent sugarless organic seasonal jam. I'm a snob for good manners and for people who see the world around us.

What makes you cross?
I'm very unhappy about stupidity and ignorance.

TERRY KALJO
The Memory Maker

To understand how to make a holiday letting desirable you need to understand what desirable is. Terry Kaljo knows this all too well and could best be described as a desire-ist. From Rockridge's chic façade (Rockridge is the Elle Macpherson of the house world: older, in her forties, sun-kissed but still got it) to the purity of Bedarra Island Villa and its response to nature, Terry's trademark is on every property she lists. ▲

My work is all about . . .
Making the best of my day. I feel wonderful
when I've made great use of every hour.
You could say I'm useful and I love pleasing
people. Fortunately, my career has exposed
me to beautiful and creative things –
fashion, photography, interiors and hotels.

If I were a flower, I'd be a bunch of . . .
Happy sunflowers.

My favourite colour is . . .
Butter yellow. I fell in love with a certain
Pantone shade at last year's Milan furniture
fair and I'm using that specific shade as
a highlight in my interior architecture, clothing
and flowers for my dining room table. Privately
I love the leather and silver combo – I'm drawn
to the 'bikie chic-k' sensibility, even though
I only ride a Vespa.

I know it's daggy but I love . . .
A good cup of tea and the newspaper in bed.

My lounge at home is . . .
White linen, with removable covers so the odd
stain you can't explain doesn't matter. It's adorned
with goose-down cushions and is large enough for
two to fall asleep on after a dull movie.

What's the most played song or set on your iPod?
I love Latin music and I adore sexy tango music.

What makes a house special?
You know as soon as you walk through the
front door whether a house is a home and
whether it's special. We spend half our lives
in our nest, called home, so I believe we
should make the most of it.

My dream holiday goes something like this:
The anticipation of a holiday is where the
fun begins. I dream of lying under a palm
canopy on the white sands of Bedarra Island
long before I book the flights. I can taste the
vintage Veuve Clicquot before I set foot on the
Champs-Elysée. I'm embarrassing my children
with my tango moves in the wide aisles of
Woolies long before I'm at the *milongas* of
Buenos Aires. Don't be careful what you wish
for, because believe me it will happen!

If I weren't me, I'd be . . .
My granddaughter Miya. As she was born in
2011, she's sweet, pretty, clever and has her
whole life ahead of her. I'd swap tomorrow.

My favourite charity is . . .
As an animal lover I'm on the board of the
Taronga Zoo Foundation, and as a lover of dance
I'm on the foundation board of the Sydney Dance
Company. I also support children's charities and
the Bobby Goldsmith Foundation.

My favourite animals are . . .
Beautiful birds! I'm a huge lover of hand-
reared exotic parrots, particularly the eclectus
parrot – they're so clever and sweet, sort of like
dogs and cats that can talk to you. It must run
in the family, as my son, Ash, owns a pet shop
that specialises in birds, called Birdsville.

Who are your pets?
A chihuahua called Astro Boy and pug
called Romeo.

Tell me a thing, or some things,
I didn't know about you.
I'm 'naughty'.

NATHALIE AGUSSOL

The Clothes Horse

My assignment on one of my first work trips to New York was to shoot Nathalie and her family at home. French-born, now Australia-based, she has incredible style, knows her strengths and executes them exceptionally well. I love working with fashion stylists as they, like interior stylists, work with the basic foundation of colour and shape – and the rigour they bring to these two aspects defines their flair. Nathalie's views on fashion and home are both timeless and beautiful. ▲

My work is all about...
Fashion in photographs.

What gets you up in the morning?
Coffee ... (addicted).

If I were a flower, I'd be a bunch of ...
Peonies.

I know it's daggy but I love ...
Pyjamas.

Seaside or meadows? Sweet or savoury? Sparkling or still?
Seaside. Sweet. Bubbles.

My favourite colour is ...
Electric blue.

I like to use ...
The sofa.

Where do you go for inspiration?
The art gallery.

What's your best décor or design advice?
When in doubt, leave it out.

Home is ...
My cocoon.

My dream holiday goes something like this:
**Greek island. Sun. Black rocks.
Deep blue water. White houses.**

Describe your design process.
It hatches out from nowhere ... And grows.

What's the best thing to eat in Melbourne?
Rose dessert at the Press Club.

I'd spend my last decorative dollar on ...
A lamp.

If I weren't me, I'd be a ...
Singer.

List some titles from your reading stack.
▶ *The Virgin Suicides* by Jeffrey Eugenides
▶ *Middlesex* by Jeffrey Eugenides
▶ *Vogue Paris*

Anything else you'd like to share?
The way I see it, what's truly modern and luxurious now is what was once the norm. Those who still work and create with integrity to what they truly believe in are the ones who still show respect for quality. They have the knowledge and understanding of values that are rapidly losing ground in this fast-turnaround world we've become accustomed to. Integrity is what produces good-quality furniture, good photographs, good clothes, good design in general!

CHELSEA DE LUCA

The Bedazzler

Where do you go for inspiration?
Sometimes the smallest things serve as my biggest inspiration. Books, films, photographers such as Mert and Marcus, and Ellen Von Unwerth, travels and interiors all inspire me.

What's your best décor or design advice?
Be true to your own style, and surround yourself only with pieces you love and that really reflect you – it will show.

My dream holiday goes something like this:
My dream holiday was living in Italy in a *rustico* for six months with my husband. We spent much of our time immersed in the culture, visiting family and eating and drinking some of the best food and wine in the world. I'd like to do that all over again.

I'd spend my last decorative dollar on . . .
De Gournay hand-painted wallpaper, white peacock taxidermy to perch on top of my marble fireplace and Megan Morton's design expertise.

List some titles from your reading stack.
▸ *Shantaram* by Gregory David Roberts
▸ *The E Myth Revisited: Why Most Small Businesses Don't Work and What to Do About It* by Michael E. Gerber
▸ *The Art of War* by Sun Tzu
▸ *The Great Gatsby* by F. Scott Fitzgerald

Tell me a thing, or some things, I didn't know about you.
I grew up on a banana plantation in North Queensland. I have as much an obsession with interiors as I do fashion, and interiors often serve as an inspiration for my designs.

My work is all about . . .
Creating timeless costume jewellery pieces with soul that can still be worn in many years to come.

What gets you up in the morning?
My working day usually starts at 5 a.m. with a good strong coffee, a big to do list, and above all a passion and love for what I do.

If I were a flower, I'd be a bunch of . . .
Peonies. Truly my favourite flower in the world. And it was also my wedding flower, so it holds special nostalgia for me.

I know it's daggy but I love . . .
Bonsais. Major obsession. To me, they're little sculptures of living art.

My favourite colour is . . .
Any and every shade of blue.

I like to use . . .
My paper diary – it's old school but nothing beats writing things down! – and my nonna's Italian recipes. I make her gnocchi and pasta over and over again, hoping that one day I'll perfect her dishes.

Brisbane people – they're just shinier than most. I'm a Queenslander and wear my pineapple proudly. I could impress you with plenty of other fabulous Queenslanders but you'll discover them for yourself – they're everywhere and all super-clever. There's something about growing up in strong sun, with big open verandas, breezeways and little traffic. Born and bred in Queensland, jeweller Chelsea de Luca is, well, very Chelsea de Luca. Glamour, deco and old-school femininity are her hallmarks, not in a shabby way but more informed by historical references and social context. Speaking of Brisbane jewellers, meet another one here (see page 24). She's crazy for geometry and Greek mythology. I tell you, there's something in the Brisbane water. ▲

MONIQUE GERMON
The Tale Teller

Getting to know Monique Germon is a gift. Layer upon layer, she reveals her cleverness. Not just through her film work (which is, of course, beautiful), but more in the way she takes to everything: considered, poetic, both dramatic and restrained at the same time. What's so great is that through STORY, her online store, the wider world can experience her delicate way of seeing and dreaming. The store trades not only in beautiful things but also in the art of storytelling. In Monique's words: 'Story reveres authenticity above all & pays homage to this as a style unto itself. Most importantly, we honour the act of storytelling as an art form.' She's managed to do something no other online trader has yet done – leave the visitor with a feeling they have every right to be there, fossicking, rummaging and fooling around among all the beauty she's created. The fact you can buy things is a bonus, I think.▲

My work is all about ...
Storytelling – history, memory, economy and the poetry of the plain.

What gets you up in the morning?
Curiosity, love and desire.

If I were a flower, I'd be ...
One of the ones that open at night.

I know it's daggy but I love ...
*M*A*S*H*, always have.

My favourite colour is ...
Black. All the best things are black.

Where do you go for inspiration?
Small country towns.

What's your best décor or design advice?
Humanism plus the law of least effort – that is to say, just be yourself and fuck trends. If you're after beauty, I'd suggest closing your eyes instead of reading blogs. Like the fate of woodcut letters and vintage props in retail, if you only follow fashion your space will be just be part of a common aesthetic that will satisfy for a season at most. One of the greatest gifts to have and to share is literally a room of one's own. I'd choose Mirka Mora's home over a Milan showroom any day. Stories spill off the walls of such houses, and then into you and your guests – osmosis at its best.

Home is ...
Where I was born – Camden, New South Wales. Camden in the 1970s was the Magic Faraway Tree of the west and the sweetest place on earth.

My dream holiday goes something like this:
Straight to New York City to work on a Woody Allen feature and see him play clarinet at The Carlyle, then a road trip across the country starting with Transcendentalist territory (especially Walden Pond and the Nearings' old place). Then through Kansas (via Wichita) and over to Monroeville, Alabama, where Harper Lee invites me over and we discuss *To Kill a Mockingbird* on her porch till the cows come home and/or my heart explodes with joy.

Describe your design process.
Head tilted slightly to the left, squinting and staring into space.

What does a working day look like for you?
Tea, walk, emails and a visit to Exeter General Store & Café to post parcels for STORY, exploring, talking into my voice memo and making many, many notes along the way.

Two skills I'll put to use this week:
▸ Writing music for a short film.
▸ Translating a feature script into a visual format, words into matter – delicious!

What's the best thing to eat in Sydney?
Yum cha.

I'd spend my last decorative dollar on ...
Bedclothes and mangle cloth from a store such as dear Peppergreen Trading, recently closed. Many new stores and stylists have been inspired by its legacy. The owner, Carina Cox (the epitome of honour), was my mentor for just over a decade and I treasure all that she and Peppergreen gave and taught me.

If I weren't me, I'd be a ...
Full-time explorer.

List some titles from your reading stack.
Everything by Robert Dessaix, Helen and Scott Nearing, Henry David Thoreau, Oliver Sacks, Christopher Hitchens and Stephen Fry.

Tell me a thing, or some things, I didn't know about you.
Professional: I used to sing with the Sydney Philharmonia choir and make quite a good living regularly singing two verses of 'Amazing Grace' at Japanese weddings – hilarious.
Personal: When I was little I had a pet owl that fell out of her mum's nest outside my bedroom window. I think about Misty to this day.

Draw your self-portrait.

Anything else you'd like to share?
One day, if you can't find me online, know that I'm happily tending my family, my friends, my piano, acres of vegetable gardens, chooks, books and cherry trees.

PEOPLE I LOVE

BECI ORPIN

BECI ORPIN

The Story Teller

My work is all about . . .
Drawing pictures, dreaming, making things look nice, having fun.

If I were a flower, I'd be a bunch of . . .
Billy buttons.

I know it's daggy but I love . . .
Vegemite on toast.

Seaside or meadows? Sweet or savoury? Bubbles in wine?
Seaside, sweet and bubbles, please.

My favourite colour is . . .
Yellow – all shades.

I like to use it . . .
In little bits and pieces.

Where do you go for inspiration?
Nature, my library or local op shop.
My kids and friends are good, too.

What's your best décor or design advice?
There's nothing wrong with a bit of clutter in the right places.

Home is . . .
Messy, most of the time.

My dream holiday goes something like this:
Breakfast picnic and bushwalk at Wilson's Promontory, spot of shopping and lunch in Tokyo, an afternoon ocean swim at Langkawi Island, a taco dinner in Mexico, cocktails and late-night snacks in New York.

Describe your design process.
Lots of thinking, lots of research, then scribbling, drawing, painting, cutting, pasting and computering. Repeat until happy.

What does a working day look like for you?
It's hard to tell when it starts and stops, but it usually starts with coffee, then emails, some playing in my sketchbook, drawing on the computer, checking a few blogs and looking at some books. Then some more emails.

Two skills I'll put to use this week:
▸ Getting two kids showered, dressed and fed, with their lunchboxes packed, and off to school in under thirty-five minutes.
▸ Writing and crossing off lists.

What's the best thing to eat in Melbourne?
Burrata from La Latteria, bread from baker D. Chirico, broad beans from my garden, anything made by Raph (tacos and burgers in particular).

I'd spend my last decorative dollar on . . .
Too hard!

If I weren't me, I'd be a . . .
If human, a botanist; if not human, a bird – a welcome swallow.

List some titles from your reading stack.
▸ *Nobody Told Me There'd Be Days Like These* by Amanda Maxwell
▸ *Nella Notte Buia* (*In the Dark of the Night*) by Bruno Munari
▸ *In Defense of Food* by Michael Pollan
▸ *No One Belongs Here More Than You* by Miranda July

The good life is . . .
Hanging with my fam, holidays and work satisfaction.

Tell me a thing, or some things, I didn't know about you.
I'll always be a hippie child at heart. I really like birdwatching. I'm addicted to riding my bicycle.

What would be your other career choices?
Botanist or midwife.

Do you believe in horoscopes?
I was fanatical about them as a kid – I had all kinds of books and knew everything about them. These days I'd like to believe in the universe as a higher power, but I think it's broader than horoscopes.

I met Beci and her beautiful boys through a magazine shoot. She was the perfect subject: she bought us top-notch coffees, showed us around and left us alone to discover all the incredible booty stashed in every corner of her place. Her home is her work studio and is filled with life and fun. So much so, I was convinced that she and her husband, Raph, were the type to put bubble wrap under their floorboards – every time we walked from studio to home area, there was a super-loud 'pop/squeak' sound. That's the kind of place it is. You believe they have, for a giggle, laid bubble wrap under the floor! But it really was just an odd floorboard squeaking on its joist. ▲

RACHEL ASHWELL
— *The Revamper*

There was a time when shabby chic ruled the world and, like all trends, made flowery way for the next extreme trend. I've always admired Rachel Ashwell's personal take on home – so nurtured, so comfortable, so pleasing. I'm chuffed that she's managed to take her shabby chic to a new level since its downturn. You can sleep on her sheets, upholster your flea market finds (or, even better, buy hers) and stay at The Prairie, a B&B of shabby chic proportions. Want to relax a room? Hand me a shabby chic faded tea-stained rose and problem solved. ▲

I know it's daggy but I love . . .
I'm not sure what that means but I do love that all the art cards my kids made tell me how beautiful and perfect I am (haven't received one in a few years).

My favourite colour is . . .
Hmmm. Hard. White is my neutral wow but I'd be lost without the romance of pink . . . and then smoky teal adds a handsome but meaningful layer. I like to use this palette wherever I call home.

What's your best décor or design advice?
Learn what works for you – there's no point creating someone else's dream home. It may take you time to work out what's right, but it's worth it. Try to blend in existing pieces, even if you have to repaint or reupholster. Choose a theme and try to blend everything together. Go slow, but not so slow that you never make your home.

online communications. Because I passionately want to get my true voice across all that I do, I take much time to speak with words that carry my aesthetic. There are flea market days (usually at the B&B) that I love, searching for treasures. There are design days that I love, where the collaboration of vision and execution comes into play.

What's the best decorating material?
It would have to be wood: an old wooden dining table, wine-glass rings, engraved initials, all evidence of gatherings before and stories told.

If I weren't me, I'd be a . . .
Mentor to young kids, I'd like to think. I love the innocence before life makes everything too scary.

My lounge room at home is . . .
A hotchpotch room of tattered elegance. A huge Rachel Ashwell Shabby Chic Couture velvet sofa with vintage pillows. Two mushy swivel chairs that turn towards a ginormous fireplace with a hotchpotch of art pieces on the mantel. A couple of faded vintage rugs. Books. A twinkly chandelier and wall sconces with threadbare shades. A wooden wardrobe rack with an eclectic mix of future fabrics and apparel. My favourite ever robin's-egg blue Texan big, big cabinet. Two little Spanish gold-painted chairs with woven seats. It's a yummy room.

Tell me a thing, or some things,
I didn't know about you.
I'm shy, very introspective and struggle with the pace of the world today. My ability to create homes and products of such romance and substance is due to forever striving to create home, a place that's safe and where time stands still. The void of life fuels my vision and passion.

How do you stay relevant?
My hope is, with our big little company, my ongoing writing, our products and the experience of the B&B, that we can continue to offer a tactile and authentic lifestyle with a backbone of someone who cares passionately about being of substance and real.

am holiday goes something like this:
y Ireland or Wales, maybe the English
yside. Rain and wellington boots, open
e, a piano and guitars around. Flea
s at the weekend to rummage through.
tove to make big roast dinners, and lots
s to read and art supplies to use. Friendly
urs nearby and a comfortable cottage.

be your design process.
my biggest inspiration. I wonder if I hadn't
bies if I'd ever have worked out the need
me that was beautiful, functional and
table. When I'm inspired, I have design
gs with my team, and we discuss how
fest my vision. For us, it's all about the
We never design to fill a merchandise
e only design from life's inspiration.

PEOPLE I LOVE

HENRY WILSON

The Up-cycler

It's like Henry knows what that 10 per cent extra is that will make a product go off the charts. I mean, how did he know that a glass shade would modernise the anglepoise lamp? How did he know I'd love my Tolix chair if it had a leather slip to meet the hard galv? How does he make repurposing so exquisite? I mean, is he psychic or something? No, he's Henry Wilson, and as far as home-grown design goes he's one to watch on the world map. Trust me. ▲

My work is all about . . .
Questions. Why do I need to make this? Does something better already exist? Can I use it in some way?

What gets you up in the morning?
The thought of using my coffee machine. I love the ritual. Something sweet, something bitter. It can be rewarding to love and care for a machine, especially when it's considered and well made.

If I were a flower, I'd be a bunch of . . .
Flat-leaf parsley.

I know it's daggy but I love . . .
Chutney and cheese. Together.

My favourite colour is . . .
Blue. Indigo, preferably.

I like to use it . . .
On my person.

What's your best décor or design advice?
Beauty is truth. A form that's given by investigating honesty cannot be argued with.

Home is . . .
Jumping off the rocks at North Bondi. My favourite shirt on over a back crackling with dried salt.

My dream holiday goes something like this:
Sailing: a ten-day passage across an ocean puts everything in perspective.

Describe your design process.
The most important thing I have learnt from my (limited) experience is a simple question, which I use whenever I begin a new project: Can I find a better example of this object/ system/model in existence already? If the answer is yes, then I'll examine it deeply or find a different angle. Now more than ever, you need an ethical standpoint as a designer creating more stuff.

Skills you'll put to use this week:
▸ Some form of traditional woodwork (this is my formal training).
▸ Tying a bowline knot – I may or may not use that, but I can do it behind my back.
▸ Probably flexing some computer skills – I'm building an online store with Trent Jansen, trentandhenry.com.

What does a working day look like for you?
Early rise: I can't sleep in – it's a curse. Emails and newspaper with a sticky, rich espresso, minimum milk. Drive out to see a maker or manufacturer (recently this has been a foundry – I like foundries). Lunch in the studio with some of my studio mates – this tradition of eating a proper, cooked meal with your colleagues at lunchtime is a bit of a European hangover. Emails, mock-ups, more emails, more admin, etc. If it's a Friday, possibly an arvo beer in the lane outside the studio (weather permitting). I might have a slim, perfectly rolled cigarette.

What's the best thing to eat in London?
Sharing a Thai or Vietnamese whole, fried fish with someone who agrees with your view on heat. A perfect anaemic soup filled with dumplings from Din Tai Fung. A salt-beef bagel with extra-hot English mustard and a pickle. Look for the line-up on Brick Lane, London.

I'd spend my last decorative dollar on . . .
An original rush-seated Gio Ponti Superleggera Chair or, if I couldn't find the perfect chair, I'd probably decorate my mind with some heady hallucinogen.

If I weren't me, I'd be a . . .
Tugboat captain or surgeon.

Tell me a thing, or some things, I didn't know about you.
I've sailed a totally unseaworthy boat past the Horn of Africa. I naïvely thought pirates were a myth. I eat meat as a garnish to my meals of mainly veg. I travel alone because – oddly – it gives me a sense of place. I did a menswear collection for a fashion label but it didn't work out due to manufacturing costs in Australia. Now I wear all the samples.

Anything else you'd like to share?
For me, design is about more than simply filling the world with more objects. Instead, my work is a process of design thinking that involves careful examination of my environment and the creation of sensitive, thought-provoking responses to it. Sometimes these responses are additions to design objects, others they're new objects born from a new need. They're always, however, a response to the human, and a continuation of what science refers to as a 'body of knowledge'.

BETH & IAIN HALLIDAY

The Taste Makers

Shop-owner Beth and her architect/interior designer son Iain are Potts Point fixtures. Not because they're screaming rah-rah people – quite the opposite. Their dogs Ace and Daphne are such traffic-stoppers, it's hard for them to make it from the florist to the coffee shop without a gazillion hellos and goodbyes. Beth has a shop called Palm Beach Home, where she trades in irresistible small pieces displayed on circular creamy plinths Iain has designed for her. It's a pleasure to spend your money there, and you might get to see the dogs, too. Iain is a partner in BKH (Burley Katon Halliday architectural and interior design practice). The Hallidays are living proof that you can live with pets *and* have nice things! ▲

What gets you up in the morning?
BH: A new day.
IH: Good coffee and the gym, and my dogs, Ace and Daphne.

If I were a flower, I'd be a . . .
BH: Posy of roses.
IH: Phalaenopsis orchid.

I know it's daggy but I love . . .
BH: Passionfruit sponge at DJs.
IH: Hamburgers with fries.

What's your favourite colour or colour combination?
BH: Blue and pink.

Where do you go for inspiration?
BH: Our Palm Beach home, looking out.
IH: Paris.

What's your best décor or design advice?
BH: Use a professional.
IH: Buy fewer things but buy the best – even when you stretch too far to get it.

Home is . . .
BH: Where Iain is.
IH: An incredibly important sanctuary, a safe and tranquil place full of things and people I love.

My dream holiday goes something like this:
BH: Having time for a holiday, then to the Greek Islands and Paris.
IH: Arrive in Paris and never leave.

What's your design manifesto?
IH: Always try for the best for your client, whatever your vision is for them and even if they don't get it at first. If you try selling things you don't believe in, no one wins.

Describe your design process.
IH: Look at the client, their budget, location and wants, and try to use this as a framework for something as fabulous as I can dream up.

What does a working day look like for you?
BH: Busy.
IH: 75 per cent client meetings (many of them intense), 25 per cent design.

Two skills I'll put to use this week:
BH:
▸ Patience.
▸ Perseverance.
IH:
▸ Salesmanship.
▸ Marriage guidance counselling.

I'd spend my last decorative dollar on . . .
BH: A beautiful artwork.
IH: Flowers. Without them, most rooms are soulless.

If I weren't me, I'd be a . . .
BH: Lady of leisure.
IH: Billionaire who employed someone like me.

List some titles from your reading stack.
BH:
▸ *Kenzo* by Olivier Saillard & Antonio Marras
▸ *The World of Gloria Vanderbilt* by Wendy Goodman
▸ *Dreaming of Chanel* by Charlotte Smith & Grant Cowan
IH:
▸ *True Prep: It's a Whole New World* by Lisa Birnbach
▸ *Billy Baldwin: The Great American Decorator* by Adam Lewis
▸ *The World of Madeleine Castaing* by Emily Evans Eerdmans
▸ *Houses* by Michael S. Smith
▸ *Coco Chanel: The Legend and the Life* by Justine Picardie

What's your favourite iPhone app?
BH: Camera.
IH: I wish I was technical enough to use my phone to such advantage!

Who's on your blog roll?
BH & IH: Habitually Chic.

What's your career highlight?
BH: Opening my first shop.
IH: Opening BKH NYC and participating in the New York Kips Bay Show House in 2008.

What's the best movie for house-spotting?
BH:
▸ *Something's Gotta Give.*
IH:
▸ *Blade Runner* – Frank Lloyd Wright's Ennis House
▸ *Something's Gotta Give* – definitive Hamptons house
▸ *The Great Gatsby* (1974) – Stanford white mansion, etc.

If I were a chair, I'd be . . .
BH: An egg chair.
IH: A Mies van der Rohe daybed. So effortlessly elegant, even in the crappiest version.

Tell me a thing, or some things, I didn't know about you.
IH: I love a very broad range of styles, from antique to highly minimalist and everything in between.

BIRDS
OF THE WORLD

PEOPLE I LOVE

BENJA HARNEY

BENJA HARNEY
The Paper Engineer

Artists can be a temperamental bunch, but show Benja paper and watch him cool it right down. This isn't the curly, girly style of paper art, but paper art created from hardcore utilitarian white art paper: no fussing, no frills, just intricate cuts to make beautiful new forms. There's nothing Benja can't make out of paper, and I *mean* nothing: steaks, cucumber sandwiches, dresses, tassels, birds, steamships and cameos. Benja has spent three months in a secret Parisian studio as a guest of Hermès for its 'Petit h project'. Hooray! This guarantees that the whole world will get to witness his genius. ▲

My work is all about . . .
Passion, creativity and precision with paper.
I strive to push the boundaries of this most humble of mediums.

What gets you up in the morning?
It's either the blue sky or a deadline –
both are great motivators.

If I were a flower, I'd be . . .
An orchid from a misty valley.

I know it's daggy but I love . . .
Celine Dion. I admire her spirit – none of my friends even remotely get it, though.

My favourite colour is . . .
Something bright, often next to something brighter still. Colour makes me happy.

I like to use . . .
My hands – nothing comes close to the feeling of making something handmade.

Where do you go for inspiration?
My friends, history, art/design.

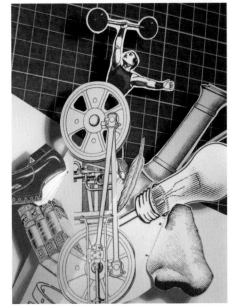

What's your best décor or design advice?
Follow your own taste. Buy bits here and there on your travels. Old and new together always works – it creates a friction.

My dream holiday goes something like this:
Stockholm/Tokyo/Bronte Beach.

Describe your design process.
I begin with thinking, then I hit my cutting mat. When you're working with paper, you just have to begin and see what comes out of your brain via your hands. I love solving design challenges with technical intuition.

What does a working day look like for you?
It usually starts early and ends late –
I find the night-time the best time to concentrate – I'm a total night owl: 'Hoot!'

Two skills I'll put to use this week:
▸ **Concentration.**
▸ **Stamina.**

I'd spend my last decorative dollar on . . .
An old treasure I found at a flea market or something by Tom Dixon.

List some titles from your reading stack.
▸ *Just Kids* **by Patti Smith**
▸ *Design as Art* **by Bruno Munari**
▸ *Designing Design* **by Kenya Hara**
▸ *The New Yorker, World of Interiors* **and** *Fantastic Man* **magazines**

The good life is . . .
Well-made shoes, laughing friends, good wine and food, and the beach.

Tell me a thing, or some things,
I didn't know about you.
I love jets – aren't they incredible machines?

CAROLYN FRASER

The Printer

For a dainty woman, Carolyn lifts some heavy-duty equipment. An incredible artisan, she's an expert letterpress- and hand-printer based in Melbourne. I wanted to meet her to fuel my fixation with stationery and all things related to it, but my allocated hour wasn't enough. She's a consummate professional and her work is a real labour of love. I walked out thinking that if I could pay triple her asking price, as I now had a small understanding of her process, I would. When she showed me the wedding, party and birth announcements she prints, I realised that she gets to help people through some of the loveliest times in their lives. When Carolyn and I met, my husband and I were lukewarm about moving house, but when I saw her 'change of address' samples, for me the deal was done. I returned from Melbourne adamant about my decision but unable to fess up that the thought of having one of Carolyn's cards was the trigger. ▲

My work is all about . . .
Craftsmanship. I love the quiet, meditative work of setting type, the bite of type into soft paper, making fine adjustments of ink and impression, checking the integrity of letterforms under the loupe, the rhythmic work of hand-feeding the press. I'll never tire of seeing something come off the press – it's deeply satisfying.

What gets you up in the morning?
Breakfast!

My favourite colour is . . .
Red. Pantone 187.

I like to use . . .
My two presses – a 1926 Chandler & Price platen press and an early 1960s Vandercook SP-15 proof press. The Eiffel Tower letter-opener I won in a high school French poetry recitation competition. My lovely bicycle – a burgundy Pashley Princess.

Where do you go for inspiration?
Bookshops. Flea markets. Long walks.

Home is . . .
A comfortable bed. Bread dough rising. Something interesting on the radio, something tasty on the stove. A half-written letter to a friend on the dining room table.

My dream holiday goes something like this:
Watching puffins in Scotland. Eating a burrito in San Francisco. Hurtling down a highway in an auto-rickshaw in India. Finding a flea market almost any place.

Describe your design process.
I like to make mock-ups and play with different proportional relationships between elements. I like to sit with an idea until it feels right.

What does a working day look like for you?
I might be at the type case or press, at my desk or at the State Library. The best days begin with a bike ride to work. Lunch is important.

Two skills I'll put to use this week:
▸ **Pulling a proof.**
▸ **Patience.**

I'd spend my last decorative dollar on . . .
Skylights.

Tell me a thing, or some things,
I didn't know about you.
When I visited San Francisco with my family at fifteen, I knew straight away that I was meant to live there. At home, I doodled my name with made-up San Francisco addresses on the backs of envelopes. I was twenty-two when I moved there, ostensibly as an exchange student at the University of California, Berkeley, but I knew I'd have used any excuse to get there. Something about the place sang to me. It might have been the geography, the light, the pastel Victorian houses or the Mexican food, but I loved the place more than any other I've known before or since.

TARA BADCOCK
The Embroiderer

My work is all about . . .
Tracing histories and themes of beauty, utility, cultural identity and social/collective memory. Through a combination of textile manipulation and embroidery techniques, I seek to connect with a deeply ingrained human tradition of communicating in cloth grand and worldly ideas as well as private and intimate concepts.

If I were a flower, I'd be . . .
One of those huge starburst Chinese firework 'flower' displays in a warm autumnal night sky! Life is short and must be grasped at every transient moment!

My favourite colour is . . .
I love colour! All of it! My mother had education in colour while training as an art teacher in the 1960s and she's passed this on to me. I derive so much pleasure from playing with colour – even colours I dislike can bring life and energy to a composition when juxtaposed with the 'lovely' colours. Certain colours I return to constantly because they hold special memories and associations – a slightly faded blue–grey with a certain amount of green or a particular shade of pillar-box red. I get excited more about colour partnerships – like mulberry and pewter, mustard-yellow and storm-sky blue, crimson and pale aqua. I enjoy challenging myself and my use of colour.

Two skills you'll put to use this week:
▸ **Patience.**
▸ **Determination.**

I'd spend my last decorative dollar on . . .
A 1930s silver Bauhaus candlestick.

List some titles from your reading stack.
▸ *The Elegance of the Hedgehog* by Muriel Barbery
▸ *Boating for Beginners* by Jeanette Winterson
▸ *Photocopies: Encounters* by John Berger
▸ *The Baby of Belleville* by Anne Marsella
▸ *Jamaica Inn* by Daphne du Maurier
▸ *Mrs Beeton's Book of Household Management*
▸ *Les Paradis Artificiels* by Charles Baudelaire
▸ *Le Rêve* by Emile Zola
▸ *The Unlikely Voyage of Jack de Crow* by A. J. Mackinnon
▸ *The Guernsey Literary and Potato Peel Pie Society* by Mary Ann Shaffer
▸ *The Divided Heart: Art and Motherhood* by Rachel Power
▸ *Community of Thieves* by Cassandra Pybus
▸ *Colour: Travels Through the Paintbox* by Victoria Finlay
▸ *Les Animaux de Mimi* by Lucy Cousins
▸ *The Very Hungry Caterpillar* by Eric Carle
▸ *Three Bags Full* by Leonie Swann
▸ *The Art of Travel* by Alain de Botton

Just when you think everything's mass-produced, along comes Tara Badcock, the patient maker behind Paris + Tasmania. Sometimes she's in Paris, most of the time in Tasmania, living in an old converted flourmill. She consistently delivers an admirable level of detail in her choice of silks and linens (mostly) but sometimes even denim (if it's nice and dark) or leather (which requires patience and, as she admits, a lot of hope!). Her roster of work includes love letters on pages of silk, satchels with special dates, tea cosies destined to become heirlooms, and rosettes to mark the birth of babies. Tara's work is proof of the magic that happens when you work with your hands and your heart. ▲

PEOPLE I LOVE

CAROLYN QUARTERMAINE

The Queen Bee

I'm fairly sure it was Ms Quartermaine who got my mind wandering into the world of styling. Her cursive writing printed on silks in the early pages of *Vogue Living* made my heart stop and my brain fuzzy – it truly felt a strain to draw breath. She was – and still is – all over it. She'd pop a fluoro plastic tray on a scratched-up marble top with a crystal bucket full of roses and it was like an electric shock to the eyeballs. She made the elaborate appear effortless. She made the inexpensive look like an investment. She can make a pedigree antique appear playful. If there were a Stylist Hall of Fame, CQ would have the largest tea-stained satin rosette of them all. The original is always the best. She's since moved on to textile design, where she's making just as big a mark. ▲

My work is all about . . .
Paint and paint marks and the love of colour and beauty and the accidents of paint and the energy of paint.

How did you get into textile design?
I'm a painter. I did six years at art school and a Master of Arts in a fine art area of textiles at the Royal College of Art, where I've also taught for the past fifteen years and have been made Professor of Print. My collages are made from my own printed papers and materials, so one day I pinned some collage of script to a French chair, which is where it began, and then there were shoots in my home and so I printed longer pieces and hung them on walls, mixed with paper collages. So that was the start, but already I had worked with paper and silks for years – from the late 1970s onwards, really.

What's your favourite fabric in your collection?
Probably French abstract or my *eau de nil* signature script. The script for me is still very important, as it relates to my early collages and paintings – it's where it all started.

Two skills you'll put to use this week:
Impossible! Two? Every skill is layered into another skill and linked, and so on. I deal with everything and anything: painting, collaging, transporting, designing, styling, carrying, team organisation, loading the van. If you're not there to do everything, then any project or artwork or any aspect of the work loses out. It doesn't have the same integrity, so it will never have the right impact and soul. It's hard work, but it has to be to be right.

What gets you up in the morning?
The desire to make things anew, to reinvent.

Seaside or meadows?
I love the infinity of looking at the sea, the same as lying in a meadow and looking at the sky. It's peaceful and you can dream, and then you create.

Bubbles in wine?
A glass of Pomerol.

My favourite colour is . . .
It's all about moments and phases of colour. I always return to grey and lilac shades and hues . . . There are times when I go for bursts of bright yellow/orange acidic colours but the *eau de nil*/pale greys and the colours in shadows – they are constant, as are pale English sour-pink plaster walls.

I like to use it . . .
As a background.

My dream holiday goes something like this:
A Sicilian *palazzo* with an overgrown garden, an element of Istanbul and Toyko thrown in . . . and not too far from the sea.

My favourite season is . . .
All seasons are magical. I love the changes and the longing to see that season again. I intensely adore spring because of the lightness and purity of the greens and spring flowers, summer for roses, autumn for the crisp mornings and winter for the blanket of white.

I'd spend my last dollar on . . .
Roses for someone else.

List some titles from your reading stack.
▸ *A Sport and a Pastime* by James Salter
▸ *The Woman in White* by Wilkie Collins

The good life is . . .
Simple. Very, very simple.

Do you write in pen or pencil?
Very, very fine pens. I rarely touch pencils. I have a vast array of colourful felt tips from Tokyu Hands on my tables.

What inspires you?
Oscar Wilde usually gets it right . . . and kindness is inspiring.

What kind of house did you grow up in?
I was born in a vast house from 1810 in Cheltenham, a pure Regency house. After that I moved house fifteen times, including two more countries. I am by nature now very nomadic.

Are you a good cook, an entertaining entertainer or more of an appreciative guest?
In making others feel happy you need to be a bit of all three.

What's the perfect gift for a host or hostess?
Always flowers. If possible, I'd pick the flowers from nature and mix them with branches from lemon and olive trees, jasmine and other vines, etc. It all depends which city or country I'm in as to what's appropriate. I've often stood in foreign cities on market squares rebundling vast groups of flowers and rewrapping them to get them right. Always keep a ball of string in your bag! I also give special gifts whenever I find something that will make someone happy – these moments carry more weight and memory.

Do you believe in horoscopes?
Yes, I like to believe that it works. I'm a Taurus – all the other bits of my personality are in Capricorn.

DEBORAH LLOYD

The Collaborator

Deborah Lloyd has managed to keep the 'Kate' in Kate Spade since Kate sold the business to Liz Claiborne's enterprises, but also to put in the 'Deborah' as well. Nifty-thinking, swift-moving and essentially a glamour-hound, Deborah has built on Kate Spade's playful legacy but added her own touches, beautifully intertwined with today's new media. Kate Spade the business blogs prolifically, parties like it's 1999 and considers visual merchandising its major catch. Its website is as good as its in-store experience and soon you'll be swamped with its recent infatuation turned collaboration with Florence Broadhurst. It was just a matter of time before those two joined up.▲

Our work is all about . . .
Making you smile!

What gets you up in the morning?
At the moment my new puppy, Stanley.

If I were a flower, I'd be a bunch of . . .
English garden roses.

What's your favourite colour combination?
Red and pink.

My favourite colour is . . .
Shocking pink.

I like to use it . . .
In abundance.

What's your favourite room in the house
and why?
**My parlour. I love sitting on the floor there
and reading.**

My dream holiday goes something like this:
Escaping to the Caribbean with my husband.

What makes a house special?
Laughter.

What does a working day look like for you?
**Every day is an adventure. I never seem
to do the same thing twice.**

What are your luggage preferences?
**A bag that will expand to fit
my shopping purchases.**

What was your best Australian moment?
**Seeing the Sydney Opera House and Harbour
Bridge for the first time – a bucket-list special.**

What's your favourite Florence Broadhurst print?
Japanese Floral in black and cream.

Two skills you'll put to use this week:
▸ **Negotiation.**
▸ **Inspiring others.**

List some titles from your reading stack.
▸ *Fabulous Fanny Cradock: TV's Outrageous
   Queen of Cuisine* **by Clive Ellis**
▸ *The Little Book of Perfumes: The 100
   Classics* **by Luca Turin & Tania Sanchez**
▸ *Coco Chanel: The Legend and the Life*
   by Justine Picardie

I'd spend my last decorative dollar on . . .
A piece of art.

If I weren't me, I'd be . . .
D. Lloyd – gardener and florist.

The good life is . . .
**Being surrounded by those you love,
doing something you love.**

Tell me a thing, or some things,
I didn't know about you.
**I'm very good at finding four-leaf clovers.
I've found hundreds over the years.**

My favourite charity is . . .
Women for Women.

PAULA HAYES

The Natural Artist

For more than two decades New York–based landscape artist Paula has been pursuing ideas that nurture life. Her greatest wish is to help our culture not just love the beauty of nature but care for it too. Not even all my printed and filed blog pages about Paula could prepare me for meeting her: having tea and toast rubbed in dukkah in the teepee in her Brooklyn back garden was one of the most pleasant experiences of my professional life. Nature is her muse, and Paula celebrates it every way she can. Her work is in major museums, but lucky clients enjoy backyard, rooftop and/ or balcony applications of her genius. She's the closest thing I know to a living breathing representation of Mother Earth. 'My works are only very partially an object,' she says, 'they are mostly a verb. They are transforming and hopefully create a transformative relationship – and that really is the essence.' ▲

My work is all about . . .
Revealing the beauty of connecting, caring and responding to the transformations of life.

If I were a flower, I'd be a . . .
Milkweed pod opening.

I know it's daggy but I love . . .
Rice pudding.

Seaside or meadows? Sweet or savoury?
Bubbles in wine?
Seaside and meadows, sweet and savoury, red wine.

My favourite colour is . . .
Iridescent.

Where do you go for inspiration?
Vermont woods.

What's your best décor or design advice?
Be straightforward.

Home is . . .
Here in Brooklyn, New York, with Teo, our four children and turtle, kitchen, gardens, teepee, and comfy bed with a down duvet and a super-soft Muji duvet cover.

My dream holiday goes something like this:
Just like our honeymoon: a week in Vermont at our favourite hotel, Windham Hill Inn.

Describe your design process.
Epiphany in a flash, followed by years to realise the vision; layered coordination of moving parts; an intensely detailed process – political, often tumultuous, then ultimately calming and soulful.

What does a working day look like for you?
Up at five, work till ten.

Two skills I'll put to use this week:
▸ **Visualisation.**
▸ **Attempts to remain calm through the unknowns.**

What's the best thing to eat in New York?
Organically grown food, bought at the local green market, cooked at home and served on our handmade dinnerware.

I'd spend my last decorative dollar on . . .
Sage for burning.

If I weren't me, I'd be a . . .
Wolf.

List some titles from your reading stack.
I mostly read online about politics, environmental science and UFOs.

The good life is . . .
Having clean air, water, food and a healthy family.

Tell me a thing, or some things,
I didn't know about you.
My great-great-grandmother was Chinese – I just found out last month.

Are you musical?
I play the flute.

Draw your self-portrait.
</;-)

Anything else you'd like to share?
Plants are our lifeline. Follow your heart.

JULIETTE ARENT & SARAH-JANE PYKE

The Colour Lovers

Oh, is there a colour combo these two don't like? I met them when they were starting out and I've been lucky enough to style their work for shoots. Their combined nous for unlikely alliances in the world of colour is inspired. Two heads are sometimes more powerful than one, and Arent&Pyke make potent room recipes within the Australian vernacular. ▲

Our work is all about . . .
JA: Bringing warmth, comfort, colour and beauty into people's lives.
SJP: Finding balance and creating beauty. Delivering a result that goes beyond what the client imagined for themselves.

What gets you up in the morning?
JA: The prospect of diving into the sparkling ocean down at North Bondi, shortly followed by smashed eggs and green juice from Porch and Parlour (also in North Bondi).
SJP: A blue sky and any chance of a swim.

If I were a flower, I'd be . . .
JA: I adore a beautiful bunch of flowers, but I'm always saddened when they wilt and die. I prefer them to remain in situ, like magnolias in full bloom on the tree.
SJP: A huge bunch of bright-pink peonies – so far open you know that today is their perfect moment.

My favourite colour is . . .
JA: Yellow, and always has been. Yellow was thrust upon me at an early age – in the form of an extremely bold bedroom scheme concocted by my parents. I like how yellow divides people – they love it or hate it.
SJP: Always changing, although I have an ongoing love affair with all the purples – right now it's lavender and lilac.

What's your best décor or design advice?
JA: Colour can change your life – use it.
SJP: Look for quality and authenticity in anything you buy. And take some risks! You might be sick of that amazing orange graphic fabric in two years' time, or maybe it will still make you happy every time you see it.

My dream holiday goes something like this:
JA: A month on Panarea, Aeolian Islands, Sicily, with family and friends, with plenty of eating, afternoon naps and jumping off the rocks into the *azzurro* water.
SJP: Any combination of sun, swimming and amazing food. Taking a boat around Sardinia with a group of great friends is high on the list.

Describe your design process.
JA: It usually starts with an image or an object – not one that has literal translation, but one that depicts the mood, flavour or personality of the project.
SJP: I tend to come back and forth to an idea a few times, testing it as I go. Often my first instinct is right, but I'm still working on trusting that – I tend to examine all the options first.

I'd spend my last decorative dollar on . . .
JA: A wonderful piece of slubby, stonewashed, organic-dyed Belgian linen.
SJP: Pompoms! They make everything better.

Is exercise a friend or foe?
JA: Exercise is my friend. For stamina, a clear head and a good sleep!
SJP: It's a love–hate relationship.

If I weren't me, I'd be a . . .
JA: Politician. Debating is a thrill.

What's your favourite iPhone app?
JA: The weather app. I'm always watching out for good weather – somewhere in the world.
SJP: I became obsessed with Sleep Cycle, which tracks your sleep patterns – it's strangely compelling.

Who's on your blog roll?
JA: I'm not into blogs – they completely stress me out.
SJP: Yellowtrace, The Sartorialist, Textile and Terrain, The Design Files.

What's your favourite colour combination?
JA: Grubby yellows and grubby pinks.
SJP: I'm dreaming up a scheme with mustard, grey and navy – and maybe a little hint of lilac.

What's the best movie for house-spotting?
JA: *I Am Love*, for the first scene panning over the donkey-grey and mustard-yellow carpet. Divine!
SJP: *A Single Man*.

If I were a chair, I'd be . . .
JA: A Gervasoni Ghost chair, slip-covered in soft washed white cotton.
SJP: A vintage Danish timber-armed chair, upholstered in a bold floral.

Tell me a thing, or some things, I didn't know about you.
JA: I listen to ABC Classic FM in the car. I especially like listening to Margaret Throsby when I can – she has the best radio voice.

Anything else you'd like to share?
JA: My husband finds it endlessly amusing how I describe colours: ice mint green, stormy grey, pomegranate red, lemon-tart yellow. He's a graphic designer – such descriptions are not applicable in his world.

MARTYN THOMPSON

The Collector

He is special. And so is the way he sees the world. Australian-born photographer Martyn Thompson creates pictures that make captions seem superfluous. And they are. His pictures are narrative as well as autobiographical. No more words needed. ▲

What's your own decorating ethos?
I like beautiful and I like lived-in – I'm a rustic modernist. I live and work in the same space so it can't be precious. Things get moved around a lot, often by me, so I don't like heavy furniture! I love colour – greys and greens with highlights of reds and yellows.

I know it's daggy but I love . . .
The routine in my life – for many years I travelled so much that it was hard to have regular habits and activities.

If I weren't me, I'd be . . .
Martha Graham.

Is exercise a friend or foe?
Friend. I exercise every day – it's part of my sanity-maintenance program!

Are you a pet person?
No, but I think cats are cute.

What are you most excited about?
That work and life are still evolving and there are always new and challenging things to do.

The good life is . . .
Loving the everyday.

Tell me a thing, or some things, I didn't know about you.
I spend an inordinate amount of time getting dressed.

My work is all about . . .
I couldn't do the same thing all the time – sometimes I work alone, sometimes with many other folk, some days it's taking photos and others making cardboard sculpture, sewing clothes or curating a show. Generally I love craft – I love using my hands and I'm learning to love technology, so long as that's in someone else's hands . . .

Describe your design process.
I think that most of the best stuff comes out of some sort of accident, so I'm regularly sabotaging whatever I'm working on in order to create something new, which often involves some sort of physical attack on my work. I think the most creative moments come from the gut.

Two skills you'll put to use this week:
▸ Intuition.
▸ Experience.

Tell us about your 'flashlight project' and its origins?
Last year I started doing themed 'pop-up' art shows with friends and other artists under the banner of The Tree. In December we held one in the dark and gave everyone a torch to view the work, an idea I pinched from Zenith Virago, who had done the same thing at a show in Mullumbimby – as did the Surrealists, apparently, back in the 1920s.

Where do you go for inspiration?
I don't consciously seek inspiration – it's often an amalgam of memories past or just arrives mid-conversation with others.

What's your best décor or design advice?
Mix it up, and don't be afraid of what you love.

KITIYA PALASKAS

The Crafter

Kit creates her own brand of simple, ever-cheerful loveliness in the form of paper products, piñatas and party apparel. She's self-taught but with skills underpinned by years at art school. Welcome to her world – she really does live like this! ▲

What's something no one knows about you?
I have an irrational and crazed fear of frogs. I can't even look at a photo of one without getting an actual physical reaction. I get tingly under the fingernails! It's absurd.

Home is . . .
My super-tiny, super-cute art deco apartment in Darlinghurst, Sydney.

What's the best song to make things to?
Anything by Fleetwood Mac.

What's the ultimate piñata shape?
I love traditional piñatas – the round ones with streamer-tipped cones.

Do you have a middle name?
Unfortunately not. But when I was in high school my friends thought I needed one, so they gave me the middle name Ayesha, which I quite like.

What's your favourite possession?
A very tattered plush Spot the Dog toy. He was put in my crib when I was one day old and I've loved him ever since.

Happiness is . . .
Stripes, sequins and cake.

Who's on your blog roll?
I'm never not reading Big Things (bigbigbigthings.com), Gems (lookatthesegems. com), All Daily Report (www.alldailyreport. com), Weekday Carnival (weekdaycarnival. blogspot.com.au), Gatopoder (ihatemyacne. com/gatopoder), Oh Geronimo (ohgeronimo. wordpress.com), Hank & Hunt (hankandhunt. com) and Peaches + Keen (peachesandkeen.com).

Are you an animal person?
Yes! But living in a small apartment means I can't have a pet, so I've collected an array of life-sized porcelain cats and so now I have them instead.

If you could go anywhere on holiday, where would it be?
Back to the little apartment in Brooklyn I lived in for a month two summers ago. I rode a bike everywhere, wore little shorts and huge glitzy earrings, went to many parties on rooftops, and ate mangos with hot sauce from street vendors every day like in a movie. Best. Summer. Ever.

LUCY FEAGINS

The Blogger

What gets you up in the morning?
The endless treasure hunt!

If I were a flower, I'd be . . .
A Flower Drum LOVE BOMB!
(see page 126).

My favourite colour is . . .
Chartreuse acidy yellow. Cannot get enough.

I like to use it . . .
In the bathroom. I love those fantabulously
soft Bellini Luxor organic cotton towels,
which come in the most perfect acid-greeny/
yellow shade – especially fab in combination
with sexy dark-grey/charcoal tones.

I know it's daggy but I love . . .
Country Road.

What's your drink?
Prosecco.

My lounge at home is . . .
My lounge? You mean my sofa? It's a Nook
by Jardan. It's the biggest single investment
item in our home and worth every penny –
100 per cent handcrafted in Melbourne.

**What's the most played song or set
on your iPod?**
Amy Winehouse's 'Valerie'.

**What's your favourite room
in the house and why?**
The bedroom. I live in a teeny-tiny two-room
house – the bedroom is my sanctuary. It's the
only room where I can escape the computer
and the TV. It faces west, so it gets the most
beautiful warm low light in the afternoon.

What does a working day look like for you?
If I'm good, the following: up at 6 a.m.;
gym at 6.30 a.m.; home at 7.30 a.m.; breakfast,
coffee, then at my desk 8.30 a.m. Email, email,
email, then perhaps a meeting or two with an
advertiser, a designer I'm interviewing, a new
brand I'm profiling. Lunch on the run, then
perhaps a house shoot in the afternoon –
either on my own, with my trusty tripod in tow,
or with a photographer I've roped in for the day.
Pick up fresh fish from Canal seafood in
Fitzroy on my way home. 7 p.m. get home,
cook dinner and have an hour's face time
with the poor neglected BF; then back to
work at 8.30 p.m. till about midnight or
so – downloading pics, generating content,
uploading the following day's post. If I'm
not good, I eliminate the gym, and replace
the fresh fish with Indian takeaway :)

In three words my living room is . . .
Tiny, considered, cluttered.

I'd spend my last decorative dollar on . . .
Frank & Mint linen sheets and pillowcases.

Who's on your blog roll?
Keke (youfoundkeke.com), Melbourne artist
Kirra Jamison's love letter to Japanese cuisine;
Line × Shape × Colour (lineshapecolour.
blogspot.com), a stunning travel/photo blog
by a Sydney textile designer; Gary Pepper
Vintage (garypeppervintage.blogspot.com) –
I'm new to fashion blogs but this one is
so beautiful and the perfect snapshot of
Australian style; Oh Joy (ohjoy.blogs.com),
saccharine American eye-candy cuteness;
Design*Sponge (designsponge.com),
because everyone needs a career hero.

**Tell me a thing, or some things,
I didn't know about you.**
I don't get Facebook.

My favourite charity is . . .
ASRC – Asylum Seeker Resource Centre
in Melbourne (asrc.org.au) – an incredible
independently funded initiative that supports
refugees who have little or no other support
network. The ASRC was founded and is
run by Kon Karapanagiotidis, a brilliant,
truly inspiring man.

Anything else you'd like to share?
My middle name is Clairmont!

She did it (became Australia's biggest blogger,
that is) totally by accident. Lucy Feagins was
just born one of those nosy-parker types,
but in the nicest possible way, an untrained
sleuth turned props stylist who likes sniffing
out design and stuff in her hometown
of Melbourne. Powered by free blogging
software, her blog, The Design Files, reaches
more than 200 000 design-hungry people
a month. There'll be a book, a TV series and I'm
sure a radio show in there somewhere! Hers is
a paperless office but filled with loads of extra
pages to remind her of the goodness that is the
printed word. Oh Lucy, we gush you back. ▲

ALICE WATERS

The Provocateur

Before colour, before decoration, before history, before art, there's one thing – food. Alice Waters is to food what Matisse is to colour. The New World really does belong to her, and at sixty-plus, she's far from resting. Alice brought the kitchen garden to the White House but her work in the Edible Schoolyard will be her true legacy. She's known for her restaurant Chez Panisse, but before being a chef, she's a true humanitarian. ▲

My work is all about . . .
Reinventing our lives through food.

What does a working day look like for you?
HELL!

Two skills you'll put to use this week:
▸ **Persuasion.**
▸ **Determination.**

What gets you up in the morning?
The passion and dedication of young people.

If I were a flower, I'd be . . .
An apple tree in blossom.

I know it's daggy but I love . . .
Botany.

Seaside or meadows? Sweet or savoury?
Bubbles in wine?
Meadows that roll into the seaside.
To sit in the grass and watch the sea.
It's why I love Ireland. Savoury. Still.

My favourite colour is . . .
Maroon. I like to dress in it, I like to buy flowers in that colour and I like bowls that are that colour.

My living room is . . .
Empty except for books and a piano.

When and why and from whom
did you buy your piano?
My sister sold it to me in 1991 and I wanted it so my friends could play.

If your daughter, Fanny, were a boy
what would you have called him?
Marius (the other Pagnol character).

When did you move into your house?
Twenty-nine years ago.

My dream holiday goes something like this:
Rent a house on a beautiful island in the Mediterranean.

What will you eat for breakfast tomorrow?
Warm whole-wheat flatbread with hommus and pu-erh tea.

Summer is . . .
Not vacation time any more.

Winter is . . .
Intense.

Spring is . . .
Hopeful.

Autumn is . . .
My favourite.

I'd spend my last dollar on . . .
A bottle of Domaine Tempier rosé.

If I weren't me, I'd be a . . .
Milliner.

List some titles from your reading stack.
▸ *Lulu's Provençal Table* **by Richard Olney**
▸ *The Man Who Planted Trees* **by Jean Giono**
▸ *Food Rules: An Eater's Manual* **by Michael Pollan, illustrated by Maira Kalman**

The good life is . . .
Dinner with friends in a commune.

Tell me a thing, or some things,
I didn't know about you.
I'm not the only author of my books.

ROBERTO DUTESCO

The Visual Poet
_____

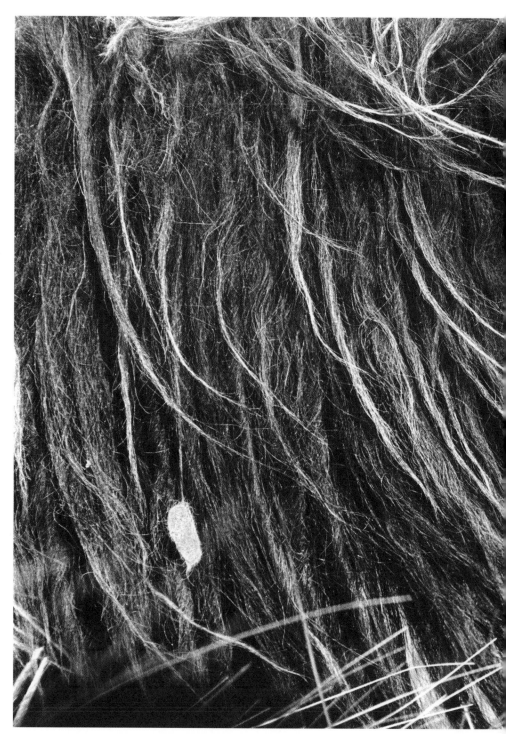

Roberto talks about people coming to the gallery and tearing up when they first see his monumental photographs of the horses of Sable Island. I was one of those visitors but I wasn't simply teary, I was outright bawling. My dad, a brave maverick of a man, one day decided to relocate us to rural Queensland. He basically picked a spot on a map that matched his price point and just did it. He wanted to ride and be around horses every day and wished the same privilege for us. Blue-ribbon riders we are not, but horse lovers we most definitely are. The emotion Roberto has captured with these animals is extraordinary, so if you're near Grand Street, Soho, pack a box of tissues and witness their magnificence for yourself. ▲

My work is all about . . .
Philosophy more than photography, poetry, sculpture, film or written effects. The medium of what I do is always related to a larger way of seeing, living, feeling and receiving all that's around, visible and invisible alike. 'Love', for example, is invisible yet all around us.

How did you meet/discover the wild horses in your photographs?
A film done by the Canadian Film Board in the early 1960s played one night, showing a place untouched by humans. I thought it must be recorded, documented and preserved for posterity. Seventeen years later it's becoming a life project.

What lessons can we learn from the wild horses of Sable Island?
Live and let live. Humans should leave some places aside, away from humans. Let nature live by its own rules – it's done so better than we have and has been there much longer than we can imagine.

Describe the moment you saw your wild horse photographs hanging in the gallery.
I've always wanted to recreate my experience on Sable Island, so many of the photographs are oversized prints as big as 8 by 12 feet. Ultimately it's the people walking into the gallery deciding what it's like, and over many years I've seen many of them emotional, with tears in their eyes. And that should say enough.

If I were a flower, I'd be . . .
The enduring bamboo.

I like to use . . .
Film and old cameras. And still do.

What do you do in your downtime?
I spend it in Brazil at the beach with my wife and kids or with friends, enjoying good stories, great food and great red wine, with golf and Cohibas (cigars).

My last meal would be . . .
If in a restaurant, probably Milos in Montreal or New York City, or a simple one in Rhodes, Greece.

What are your music tastes?
The electronic music of the 1970s and 1980s, Tangerine Dream especially. Peter Gabriel's *The Last Temptation of Christ*.

If I weren't me, I'd be . . .
Someone new, continuous and divinely aware.

I'd spend my last decorative dollar on . . .
A hut by the sea.

List some titles from your reading stack.
Mostly ancient philosophers. The book I'm reading now, *The Lost Empire of Atlantis* by Gavin Menzies, is an eye-opener!

Do you believe in horoscopes?
Don't you?

Draw your self-portrait.
A continuously changing, curious person willing to take risks and explore much and everything.

THINGS

I LOVE
TO DO

Stylists
are doing
one thing one day,
another the next
and by week's end
have been asked
to attempt
the impossible!

Seriously, one week went like this: tell a supermodel her kitchen isn't up to scratch; make a blanket appear as if it's worth parting with a month's salary; make good a broken table leg in ten minutes; build a fake wall (and paint and paper it, too); and train a peacock for a wedding. Really, stylists have to be able to do a bit of everything. That doesn't mean you can master one thing, but more that you need to have a genuine interest in most things. In short, you need to nod yes when your mind is saying, 'Oh noooooo!'

But herein lies why it's the most exciting job in the whole wide world. While your mind's telling you it's impossible and, like a reality show without a prize, the client's clock is ticking, the no really does turn into a yes.

From these hairy, scary but ridiculously exciting times, I've compiled a list of random things I'm now good at. I share them here because you truly never know when someone might ask you to take the crinkle out of a ribbon, communicate with a right-brain person or fold a fitted sheet! In a world where Google can seemingly answer every question, sometimes an old-fashioned trick or two can make you feel like a domestic hero. Trust me, they're all great to know.

All of them, however far they may be removed from your everyday life, have something to do with your hands. I find that working with your hands brings fulfilment and a real sense of accomplishment. And using traditional home arts is a way to simplify our complex lives. ●

HOW TO
JUDGE FOUND OBJECTS

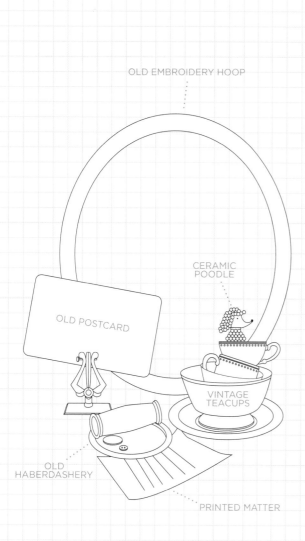

OLD EMBROIDERY HOOP

CERAMIC POODLE

OLD POSTCARD

VINTAGE TEACUPS

OLD HABERDASHERY

PRINTED MATTER

HOW TO
ANTIQUE UP A MIRROR

Man Ray was an American who spent most of his life in Paris, fighting 'blind attraction' to technical skill and craftsmanship. He wasn't against these qualities per se, he just didn't believe they should be the exclusive criteria for judging beauty. Smart Man Ray. It's him we have to thank for our deep exposure to the beauty of the everyday: the unwanted shoe, an empty matchbox, even a baguette could constitute an *objet d'art* in Man Ray's eye.

Magritte, Duchamp and Picasso were also masters of turning 'worthless junk' into items of wit and beauty. And Caravaggio – the mere sight of his name makes me giddy! These men knew that an item's price or provenance is related to the power of its form. And here's where the stylist's job kicks in: the pursuit of things that are simply beautiful, no matter what their purpose.

Next time you're feeling stuck at a junk shop or a flea market, just imagine you're Man Ray. This means your eyes either like it, loathe it or love it, and this is what's important when working with found objects. It's what makes the term 'one person's trash is another's treasure' so red-hot a prospect.

I love the look of a distressed mirror – there's something dignified about it. I also like the way it makes everyone look a little dreamier. I suggest you try to source an old mirror, as mirrors have to be 'de-silvered' from the back, and the new ones have a protective layer on the back that can be hard to remove.

Once you have your mirror, you need to buy the highly dangerous de-silvering materials and await their arrival via an anxious postman. The best kits are over at antiquemirrorps.com. If this is all too-hard-basket already (it does require a fair bit of diligence), another alternative is to call Melinda Trost, an artisan who specialises in distressed mirrors and can custom-make you a size. See her work at palacemirrors.com.au.

I like to use antique-look mirror on big spaces as well as small. Recently we did a little cupboard for a client's bathroom: we found the cabinet, had the mirror aged and it now looks exactly as it should. Perfect.

HOW TO MIMIC THE KATE SPADE WALL!

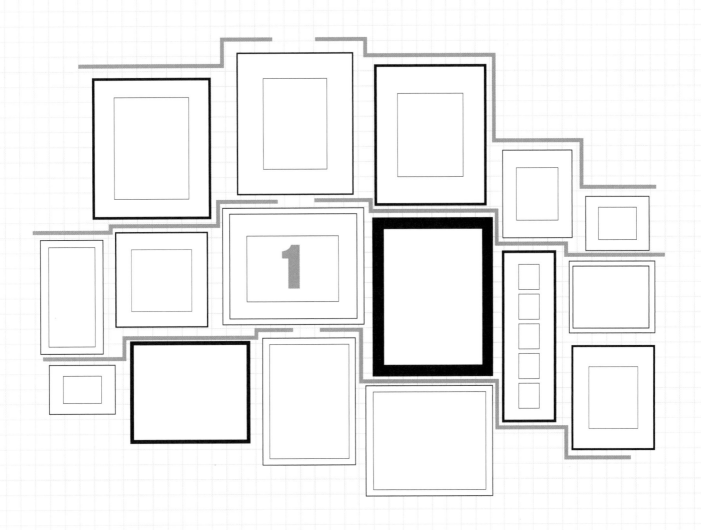

A lot of my decorating clients go to the Kate Spade store on Broome Street in New York to stock up on her charming bags, stationery and cocktail rings. They all come back squealing about the art wall in the back of the store and don't even mention the booty. But I so understand.

While it looks all random and accidental, there's a sound methodology to the wall's success. Basically, within the mix of paintings, etchings, drawings, photographs, prints and oils, there's one central, focal piece, and all the other works are mounted to 'slope' down from this one power piece.

If trying this at home, you really don't need an overly impressive centre pic. It needs to be large, but not necessarily in its subject or worth. In fact, it shouldn't be precious, as its job is to attract no attention at all. The general idea is to move from large to small as you go outwards to the edges of the wall. Try it at home with colour photocopies of all the things you'd like to hang, Blu-Tacking them into position until you get it right.

If it's any consolation, it took Andy Spade weeks to get this right after years of sourcing the individual artwork.

HOW TO
MAKE TULIPS FLOPPY

I get to work with incredible flowers and the very talented people who trade them. I've worked with everything from carnation garlands and hydrangeas (they can really hide a multitude of sins), to elegantly dancing orchids and roses flown straight from Ecuador that had to be met at the airport. I feel very lucky, as our last daughter was born on the very day that peony season arrived. Peony season is a super-short window and, due to climate change, even more unpredictable of late. Our baby, the hospital and our mantelpiece were showered with the most delicate pinkish peonies, some with heads almost the size of dinner plates. It was an incredible coincidence but, when you come to think of it, hardly one at all.

Anyway, back to the subject at hand – tulips, parrot tulips in particular. One of my favourite flower shots is a vase stuffed with floppy, droopy parrot tulips that look like they're lounging around. I'm mad for them and work with them whenever I can come tulip season (which is spring for us on the east coast). I can't wait to play host to lounging parrot tulips on my mantelpiece all September long!

In my opinion, upstanding tulips are far too Dutch-looking, so to make mine ever so slightly 'bend' down from my vase, I use a blow drier on low to soften the stems slightly. Assess the tolerance of the stem as you go, so you have a bunch that's heaving as opposed to dead! Then angle them in the vase so they all fall to the sides. Heaven! If you want to hothouse the flower open, leave the bunch out in the sun.

HOW TO
BE A REALIST

LIVING ROOM expenses record

item	$
	$
	$
	$
	$
	$
	$
	$
	$
	$
	$
	$
	$

$1   5¢   10¢ $2

While I don't like to admit it, sometimes not even throwing wads of cash at a renovation problem can fix it. The only thing that can is time. If you've allocated two weeks, plan for four. If you're renting for six months while it's being done, consider requesting an extension. Life gets in the way and, when you consider a home renovation relies on sometimes more than a dozen contractors (not to mention suppliers), you just know that however long you think it's going to take, you should double it. It will save you time in the long run, and better manage your expectations in the short term.

HOW TO DO A FRENCH HANG

Yes, the Kate Spade wall (see page 183) is by definition a French hang, but I also wanted to talk more generally about the French hang as inspiration. It originated in Parisian cafés, where struggling artists such as Renoir and Matisse gave proprietors small works in lieu of payment for food and drink. It was a win-win, it seems, creating well-nourished artists and well-dressed café walls full of small canvases that made for an interesting and energetic mix.

Art dealer Tim Olsen suggests that a French hang is not only decoratively satisfying but a great way to enter the art market, purchasing smaller works one at a time. There are many schools of thought on how best to approach it. Some like to have a theme running through the entire hang, such as a colour or subject matter, but I've seen great results where anything goes, creating a rarefied pin-board of sorts. The best thing is that you can work on it organically, adding to it until your eyes are happy and your walls are full.

Here are three rules of thumb:

❶ Start with at least five works – any fewer and you won't have enough substance to carry it further.

❷ Decide from the outset if you want to chase the same style or colour of frames, or if you're going to mix it up. (I'm a mixer-upperer – I generally find it less restrictive.)

❸ Photocopy the works and, using Blu-Tack, stick them on the wall so you can judge their size and assess the spaces between them. On that note, I like them hung fairly snugly together, as lots of space makes it feel less like a French hang and more like a lazy effort. Super-snug can also be very nice in the right room.

HOW TO WORK
WITH DECORATIVE (GOOD) CLUTTER

HOW TO OUTWIT
ACTUAL (BAD) CLUTTER

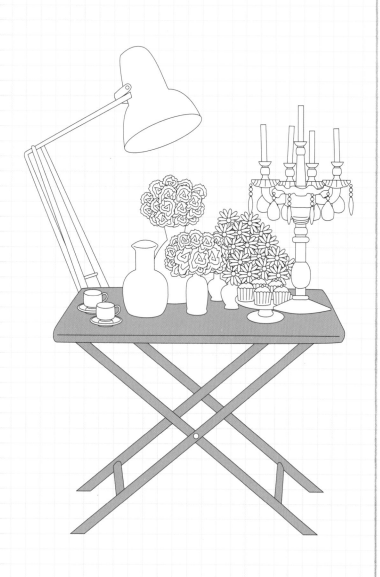

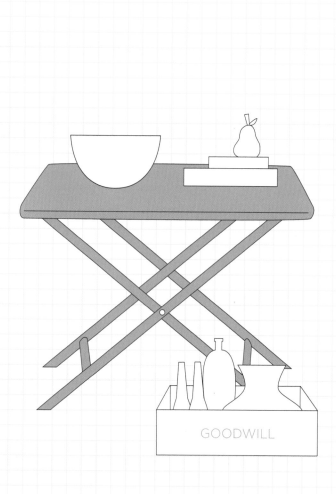

Okay, let's get this straight. First, clutter only works when its boon companion – wit – is also in the room, on the ledge or in the display nook. This is the key to it looking interesting, personal and wonderful rather than weird, odd and kooky. Secondly, as we all know, there's supreme power in union, but this doesn't necessarily mean that you can suddenly transform 'bad' clutter into 'good' clutter just by having a lot of it, or a union's worth. Last, keep an eye on clutter, even the clutter–wit successes and the clutter unions. It can really come on a little too strong, like a faint touch of garlic that overpowers the other ingredients of a recipe. Substance is what a room usually needs, not clutter.

I'm a firm believer that in any given house there are up to twenty opportunities to display your favourite things. More importantly, I'm firmly of the belief that you should take advantage of no more than four of these spaces. Big difference.

Rather than putting bits and bobs everywhere, take the opportunity to make an impact and ensure your beautiful items are viewed in their best light rather than disappearing amongst the clutter. Try organising things into room and function categories then into both style and colour categories.

HOW TO INJECT PERSONALITY INTO A ROOM

HOW TO UNDERSTAND COLOUR

WHAT NATURE TEACHES US

VARIATION IS GOOD

ONE DOMINANT + ONE SUBORDINATE = GOOD

TWO DOMINANTS = NOT GOOD

Score – you've truly made the most beautiful living room, but . . . Bust! There's one on a blog with the exact almost-same look – and it's pretty obvious you too got sucked in by the very same page 89 of *Inside Out*'s Renovation Issue. In other words, you magazine slut, you've been house-twinkied.

Don't worry. (Self-pity isn't very homelove.) Just pick yourself up and work towards adding details that will make all the difference:

❶ Combine market finds, the dodgy wedding present and a splash of a different colour to create a room no one else could copy.

❷ Don't shy away from mixing generations and styles – there's evidence everywhere that modern art and antiques are likely bedfellows.

❸ If your internal wiring allows it, don't do anything by halves. Doing it with confidence sometimes is enough to get a room through. You're always more of a decorator than you think you are.

❹ Don't for one minute think that a big budget guarantees you success. In fact, more often than not, quite the opposite.

HOW TO ADD THE RIGHT AMOUNT OF CONFUSION

I think that a home needs a little confusion and stimulation. I want to go on about this, but I know you know what I mean. You do, don't you?

Nature teaches us to expect the darkest colour value at our feet, the medium at eye level and the lightest above us, so sometimes the idea is to treat the eye and the psyche to a variation. The most successful scheme I've ever done had one dominant and one subordinate colour. My least successful schemes have had two dominants, which apart from giving no rest to the eye meant all the goodness of the other elements was lost in the tension. It was a hard lesson to learn, but one best shared.

HOW TO SOFTEN THE BLOW OF BIG DÉCOR DISAPPOINTMENTS

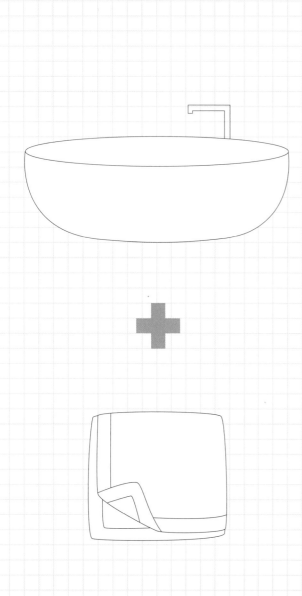

Nothing will stop bad stuff happening, but a few small things can provide comfort when it all does go bad. Installing a bath sounds like a dud recommendation, but trust me, even in space-starved Sydney, it's a gem.

I generally don't like taking baths, but about three times a year, when things go pear-shaped or haywire or I hit the wall, I draw a bath and don't resurface for at least two hours. It only takes those three soaks to pay for those 1.5 square metres of prime bathroom real estate.

Another thing I find reassuring is satin-edged blankets. Having grown up in hot Queensland, blankets are such a novelty for me. I find that waking up and stroking my toes against a satin edge is one of life's little pleasures.

HOW TO INCORPORATE A 'WHATNOT'

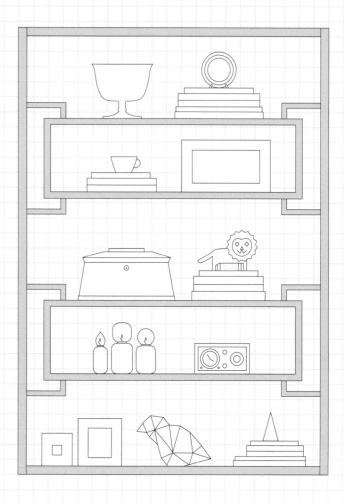

Yes, it's a word (the French call it an *étagère*), invented in the Regency period, actually, and I'm mad for it. As were the Victorians, who really loved clutter. It indicated their position in society, and was proof of their taste as well their fortune. I go into strangers' houses every day and, if I can just get a look at their 'things', I can work out who they are within ten minutes. By this I mean the little things, the things you'd want to take with you if there were a fire.

Back in the day, a whatnot was usually made of fruitwood and had a single bottom drawer with a shelf above. There was only room for the really impressive stuff on the shelf, so everything else could be concealed in the drawer. It would have been laden with Wedgwood greenware, Rockingham plates, a tea caddy and cake stands. The repetition of shape and colour would have harmonised the objects against the background of a mid-Victorian dowdy needlework carpet.

No matter how sure you are you don't want a whatnot, I reckon every home, no matter how modern, should have one. You can hide it behind sexy polyurethane doors, it can be Belgian, it can bulge under the weight of whatever it is you're into. But at the end of the day, you need an important and sacred place where you, too, can show and play with the things you're naturally drawn to, without any Victorian pretension (unless you're that way inclined!).

HOW TO MAKE A CHATTERBOX

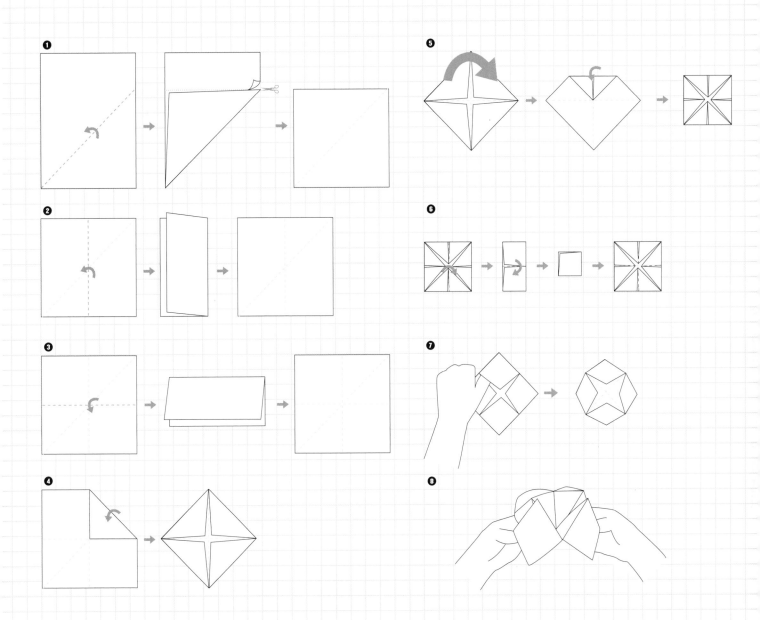

Let's not mince words: you're a total badass – you can leap tall buildings in a single bound, nail a paint swatch in one trip, command the loyalty of millions, do deals, make pasta from scratch. In short, you have great powers. But like all very powerful people, sometimes you miss out on stupid fun.

This is why I'm including this silly how-to. It's fun for birthday parties (stick it to the present instead of a shop-bought card), can make you look like a hero in front of visiting children, or will just allow you to blow an afternoon on charmingly silly paper craft. Here's how:

❶ Take a standard rectangular sheet of paper and fold the bottom edge over diagonally to meet the side edge. Cut off the strip of paper above the folded area, then unfold the paper so you have a square.

❷ Fold the paper in half from side to side. Crease the fold well, then unfold the paper.

❸ Fold the paper in half from top to bottom. Crease the fold well, then unfold the paper.

❹ Fold each corner of the square toward the centre, so the points meet in the middle and the edges of each folded corner line up with the creases in the paper. Again, crease the folds well.

❺ Turn the paper over and fold each corner towards the centre again, so that the points meet in the middle. The paper may be more difficult to fold this time, since it's twice as thick, so make sure you crease the paper firmly.

❻ Fold the paper in half to make a rectangle. Fold the paper in half again to make a square. Crease the paper and then unfold these two folds.

❼ Insert a finger into one of the folded corners of the paper and gently pull up to fluff the paper out. Do the same for the other three corners.

❽ Insert an index finger and thumb into each of the corners. Bring your fingers and thumbs together to close the paper chatterbox and pull them apart to open it.

❾ Make messages inside and under the flaps. Doodle. Draw.

HOW TO CREATE AN INSTANT CENTREPIECE

HOW TO MAKE A ROOM LOOK WIDER, AIRIER AND/OR TALLER

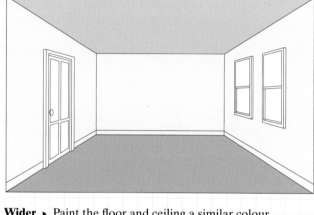

Wider ▸ Paint the floor and ceiling a similar colour and the walls a lighter colour.

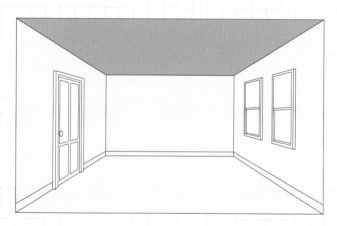

Airier ▸ Paint the walls and floor in the same pale, cool colour.

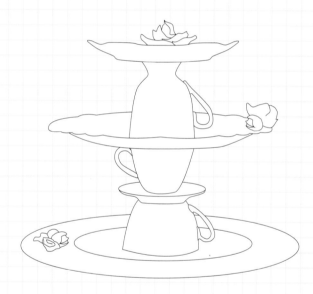

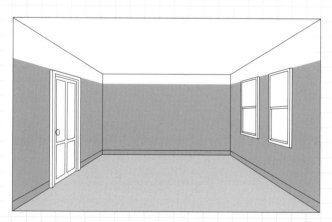

Taller ▸ Paint the walls up to picture-rail height in a soft tone, then up from the picture rail into the ceiling in white.

Pull out this quick fix for special occasions rather than every day. Assemble some of your cups, saucers, plates and jars. (You can choose to go all floral, mismatched mayhem or strictly minimal and all glass – all three work.) Build up small stacks (only risk going really high if you're prepared to suffer some breakages) until you get a nice balance. Try teacups, mugs, jars and coffee cups as the central stem with the plates and saucers as the real display. You could also incorporate a cake stand into the build. Fill the plates on top with fruits, candles, flower heads, ivy, cakes, treats or fruit.

I'm fairly firm on my stance here. No matter who you are, where you live or whatever your purse strings, the same rules apply. Choose to be either subject-focused or frame-focused. If you can confidently pinpoint the frame style you like, let this be your cue. If you're plagued by the stain, size and profile options for frames, work hard on the actual picture selection and the rest will follow.

One sure-fire way to success is a medley of faces, situations, people or places that are both close-ups and pulled back. With a wall of faces, it can be hard to focus and inject a layer of interest. You could mount some of the closer face shots with a border, leaving others (say half and half) flush with the sides of the frame.

Personally, I like a variety of frames (as long as they're of a similar nature), loosely displayed. I've had great success in the past with a photo wall where all the frames had similar coloration – in this case, all teak of various ages and designs. The same can work with all white frames or all black or all whitewashed, as a way to break up the sometimes photo-studio look of identical frames.

Basically, it comes down to whether you can arrange to have every favourite photo at the framers' at once for a mass order, or whether you prefer to go about it in dribs and natural drabs. Over to you on that one.

HOW TO DEWRINKLE RIBBON

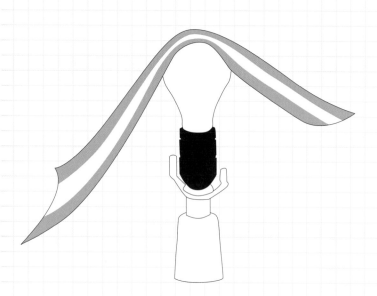

This is one of those ever so satisfying skills. If your ribbon (or any other small, delicate fabric item) has a crease or wrinkle, place it over the heat of a clean, not-long-switched-on light bulb. With your hands on both ends of the ribbon, rub it over the bulb and watch the wrinkle get steamed away.

HOW TO CLEAN A VINTAGE PAINTING

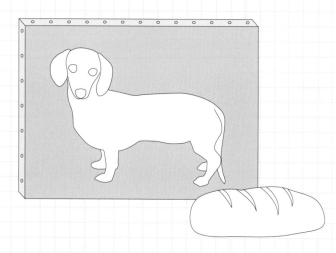

There's nothing nicer than stumbling upon one of those little almost-Danish vintage gems: fruits, a dog or even a duchess who isn't part of your family. But, given the age of the find, they're usually filthy.

Get a slice of bread or cut a bagel or roll in half. Don't use wholegrain; doughy white works best – you want the squishy white part, without the crust. Gently rub the soft bread all over the painting – don't push hard. The bread will pick up the grime like a sponge. Rub a clean piece of bread over it for a final rub-down. Done!

Now pick a spot (see 'How to do a French hang', page 185) and hang it.

HOW TO MAKE A BUNNY OUT OF A NAPKIN

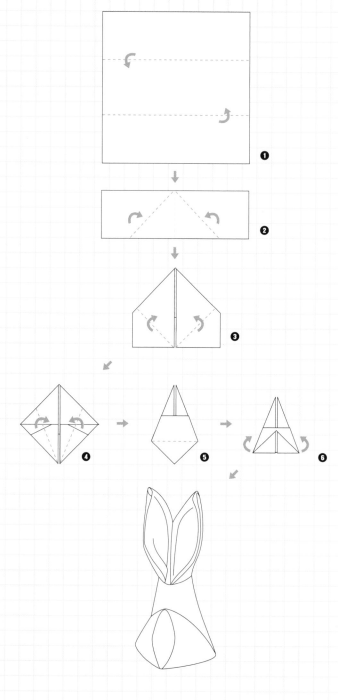

❶ Fold down the top third of a spray-starched napkin and fold up the bottom third.

❷ Fold in half with short ends together and crease along the fold. Unfold again, then fold each top corner down so that the tops line up along the fold line.

❸ Turn pointy-side up and fold the bottom up so that the bottoms line up along the central fold line.

❹ Fold the left and right points towards the centre line.

❺ Turn upside down and over, then fold the bottom point up to make a triangle.

❻ To fasten, fold the left and right corners back, then tuck one corner sideways into the pocket of the other. Pull out the bunny ears then open up the bottom and stand up.

I knew I should possibly give up styling beds when I was in a department store checking the backs of bed-linen packs and realised I'd styled almost every picture! I love working with beds and, as a result, I do know a thing or two about making them look their most delicious. My family thinks that's why my own bed is such a slob-fest: by the time I've done it for everyone else, I have no energy left to do it for myself.

The number-one thing we do in styling land that we don't do in normal-people land is put two doonas in the quilt cover. This can be two summer-weight ones (no one likes sweaty sleep) or, in winter, two medium-weight ones for instant warming. The other thing normal people don't do is gaffer-tape the backs of their European pillows to give them 'bunny ears'. When you work with beds in America you get metal tape for seriously stand-up edges!

You don't want to do this, of course, but that's why the ones in the pictures are 'up' and yours might be 'down'.

Don't forget that when you approach your bed at home, you'll almost never do so from the same angle as the camera shoots a bed – either straight-on (useful for a print or pattern at the foot of the bed) or at a three-quarter angle (which makes the bed look more luxurious). When you walk into your bedroom at home, you're higher up and the other elements in the room can catch your eye.

Lastly, it's helpful to remember that every bed in a photo has had at least two ironers going for it behind the scenes, and it can sometimes take four hours to get 'right'! This is something that should never be attempted at home!

HOW TO MAKE A BED WITH HOSPITAL CORNERS

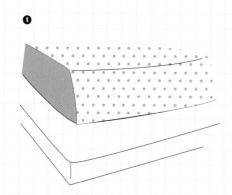

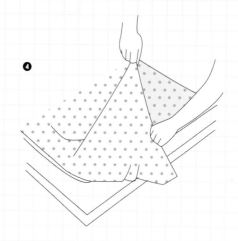

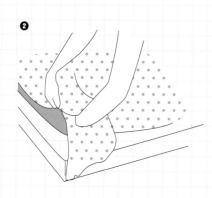

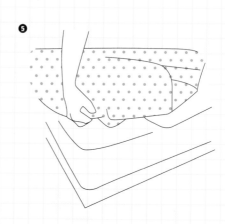

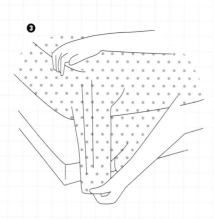

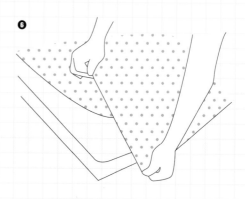

Also known as a 'mitred' corner in the styling world, a hospital corner is a super-stitched-up, highly impressive, can't-move-your-feet-around way to tuck in your flat sheet and even blankets. Here's how:

❶ Put the sheet on the bed upside down, with the top edge in line with the head of the bed.

❷ Tuck in the sheet hanging down at the end of the bed.

❸ Pick up the side edges of the sheet about 40 centimetres from the bottom corners.

❹ Pull the side up and onto the bed to make a diagonal fold. At this stage, the outermost layer of sheet should be triangular.

❺ Tuck in the little bit of sheet now hanging below the mattress.

❻ Take the bit of sheet back down off the bed and let it hang, then tuck in the bit hanging down.

❼ When you've added the blankets, fold the top of the sheet down over them and tuck in the rest of the sides.

THINGS I LOVE TO DO

HOW TO FOLD A FITTED SHEET

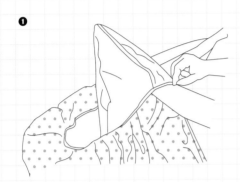

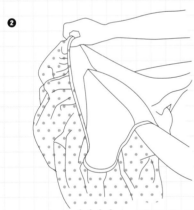

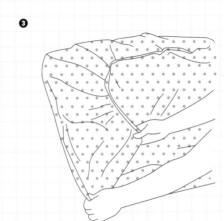

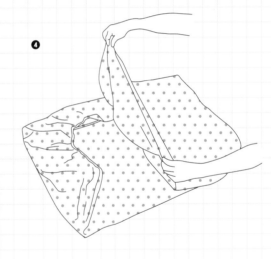

Bizarrely, I've travelled around Australia showing people this trick. I used to do it at the end of my presentations, as an ode to order and housekeeping, but people went so mad for it that I found myself practising so I wouldn't forget if stage fright caught me out. What's so good about it is that no matter how messy or unruly your house is, there's true satisfaction in knowing that at least your linen press is in order. Often, when I get home wanting to cry, I head straight to the linen cupboard, open it, inspect the loveliness, close it and sigh to myself, 'It's all going to be okay.'

Here goes. Basically, it's all in the wrist. Visit my Facebook page to see how it's done live-ish:

❶ Place your left hand in the outside of one corner of your clean, dried sheet, pushing the corner inside out.

❷ Pick up the corner at the other end with your right hand and slip the corner in your left hand into the inside of the corner in your right.

❸ Fold over the top and bottom elastic edges and smooth the creases so there's a straight fold across the top and right side of the sheet and the elastic edges form an L-shape. Repeat steps 2 and 3 at the other end of the sheet. (If you're really OC and enjoy ironing, this is where you'd add a step – iron around all sides of the now-folded sheet.)

❹ Fold the now-rectangular sheet into a smaller square or rectangle, until your folded sheet is a manageable size. (Ironers, you know what to do here.)

❺ Place in your linen press, stand back and wait for that smug sense of yes-ness to wash over you.

HOW TO
KEEP A LINEN CLOSET

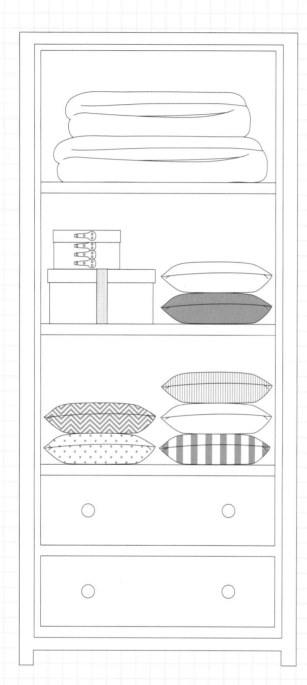

The number-one factor for achieving this feat is to master 'How to fold a fitted sheet' (see page 195). This takes care of all those exploding fitted sheets pushed into linen presses all over the world! Secondly, to achieve maximum greatness in this department, put your fitted sheets with their matching doona cover and flat sheet inside the matching standard pillowcase. This puts all components of each set within easy reach and allows you to judge your florals, stripes, prints and patterns easily. Lastly, I always wash my entire set in the same load. You want them all to fade and age at the same rate, rather than end up with a mismatched set that's as useful as a single sock.

HOW TO SPRING-CLEAN
(OR HOW NOT TO WASTE HOLIDAYS)

before   after

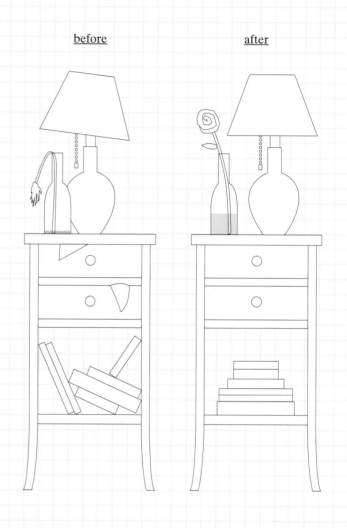

Forget New Year's resolutions – they're about as sticky as a wet Post-it. Instead, consider there are four holiday breaks a year. Dedicate each break to an area that needs editing and/or cleaning out. This way your four main dumping grounds get an annual edit and you don't ever feel overwhelmed by the prospect of cleaning out the whole house. If you have more than four holidays, you might decide to tackle two smaller rooms over the big December break.

Four is ideal, though, and mine are:

❶ the laundry and linen press, including the related present cupboard/drawer/box

❷ the kids' storage, playrooms and hobbies

❸ my own accessories, wardrobe and cosmetics

❹ the kitchen cupboards and pantry, including: stuff under the dreaded sink; dated notes, messages and sentiments stuck to the fridge; and that fully loaded third drawer down.

PS: Try to allocate the garage to someone else. It's usually heavy work, expensive and not a very satisfying place for any sort of 'before and after' action.

HOW TO DEVISE A CONGESTION PLAN FOR YOUR HOME

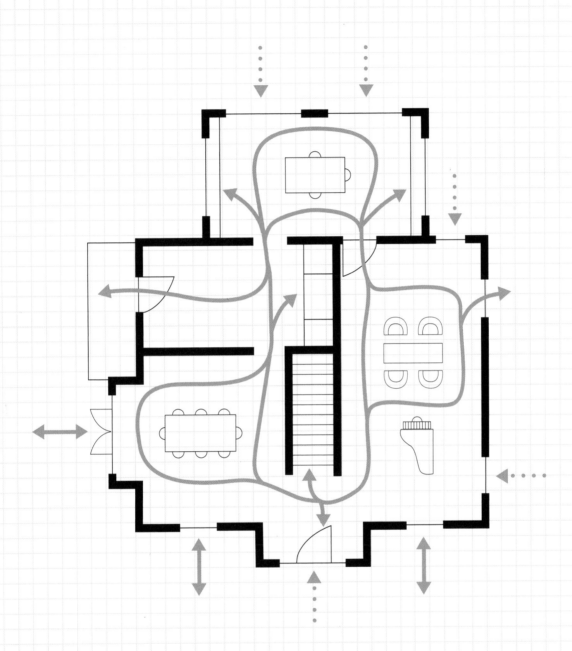

When it comes to the house, the furniture usually gets all the attention. And then it seems that we (okay, I) can talk all day about how to decorate, dress and accessorise our houses so they're magazine-shoot ready, but we forget that usability and the walk-through factor have a lot to do with a home's success.

Planning a home's circulation is truly important. Its invisible but, once you get it right, you notice the minute you enter that the space works. Get your floor plan and draw on it in blue the principal routes people make within the house. These require maximum width, as they're used by more people, so place your furniture around them and not into them. Mark less important, smaller routes in another colour and provide narrower access along these.

Trust me, it works. I borrowed this from Kevin McCloud ages ago, when I was home one day sick watching *Grand Designs* for eight hours straight. It's both the one thing I remembered and a truly treasured tip.

HOW TO COMMUNICATE WITH VISUAL PEOPLE, AKA THE SHOEBOX CHALLENGE

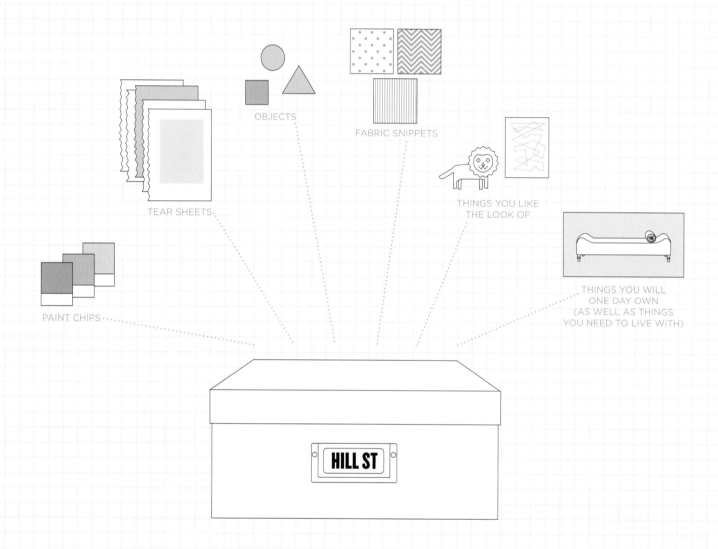

TEAR SHEETS

OBJECTS

FABRIC SNIPPETS

THINGS YOU LIKE
THE LOOK OF

PAINT CHIPS

THINGS YOU WILL
ONE DAY OWN
(AS WELL AS THINGS
YOU NEED TO LIVE WITH)

HILL ST

So you're struggling with ways to tell a decorator what you want. Why can't they just read your mind? You have stacks of magazines, hoards of books, a desktop full of reference material. This is all good. But it's not enough. When you're dealing with people who are paid to be total right-brain thinkers, you need to be able to show them your ideas in a nutshell. There's no time for misunderstandings, or you may have to live with the consequences.

Whether you're planning a new bathroom or an entire new home, grab a shoebox (or similar) and spend up to four weeks (this gives plenty of time for you to digest everything) looking for things to place in the box. This will be things you like the look of, whatever speaks to you in terms of what

you hope to achieve with the new space – it could be paint chips, tear sheets, objects, fabric snippets, ribbon, postcards, even a shell. Sometimes a tear sheet isn't really about the things within it, such as the furniture or windows, but more the feeling of the room. So with this in mind, it's important to put these non-specific tear sheets in your box, because they above all show the essence of what you want for the room.

A good go at filling the box will aid any decorative process. Handing it over is a dignified way to show what you want and can communicate much more than a wordy written brief. Be rigorous and only put in what you really do like – it's not the time for fillers and there's no prize for the fullest box.

THINGS I LOVE TO DO

Now we've dealt
with all those dinky things,
we're going into a very pragmatic
area. I believe the world is divided into
two types of people – those who like to live in
clean spaces and those who can live with clutter.
I'm the latter, but every so often (usually on about
the eleventh day of a holiday break) the disorder starts
to give me chest pains and I go into a frenzy of
cleaning, editing and producing huge kerbside piles.
Cleaning, you see, is the first step to editing, which in
my twisted mind means clearing some space to buy
even more things. So whether you're type one or
two, the urge will take hold of you sooner or later.
When it does, use the quick-look guide overleaf.
Consider it really just a present in disguise:
like when someone gives you a mixing
bowl or cleaning products –
annoying but necessary.

HOMELOVE
SEASONAL CLEANING CHART

Keeping house is a 24/7 job. Some people take it on as a full-time occupation, while others do what they can whenever they can. Regardless of your approach (some years I'm vigilant and others I'm a total badass), some things need attending to over the course of the year. In an attempt to make these must-dos a little more bearable, here they are in a likeable sunny seasonal format! ●

WINTER

GENERAL · GARDEN · KITCHEN · LIVING ROOM · BEDROOM

- Turn your mattress over
- Launder and dry-clean lightweight blankets and replace with heavier doonas and eiderdowns
- Replace summery sofa cushions and throws with heavier ones
- Rearrange pots, pans and the baking section of the kitchen cupboard
- Hose down, clean and cover outdoor furniture, and fold down umbrellas and awnings
- Wipe down all cupboard fronts
- Shake out dust from extractor fans

AUTUMN

- Turn your mattress over
- Rotate your pillows
- Flip your cushions for even wear
- Dust books and other minutiae
- Wash and rotate all your vases
- Edit the third drawer down
- Inspect and clear gutters
- Drain and store your garden hoses
- Shake, vacuum and clean rugs
- Wash curtains

SUMMER

- Turn your mattress over
- Put on your summer bedding
- Turn your mattress over
- Move your furniture around so it's in holiday mode
- Launder valances
- Wipe down all cupboard fronts
- Wipe down all power points
- Buy geraniums and put them in white (or blue and white) ceramics pots
- Buy geraniums and put them in white (so chic) throughout the house
- update the medicine cabinet

SPRING

BEDROOM · LIVING ROOM · KITCHEN · GARDEN · GENERAL

- Replace your pillows
- Turn your mattress over
- Wipe down the blades of ceiling fans
- Dust books and other minutiae
- Defrost the freezer and refreeze all ice-cube trays
- Buy a tablet for the dishwasher
- Do a quick safety inspection of any kids' equipment, tighten any bolts etc.
- Spray and degunk sliding-door tracks
- Shake, vacuum and clean rugs

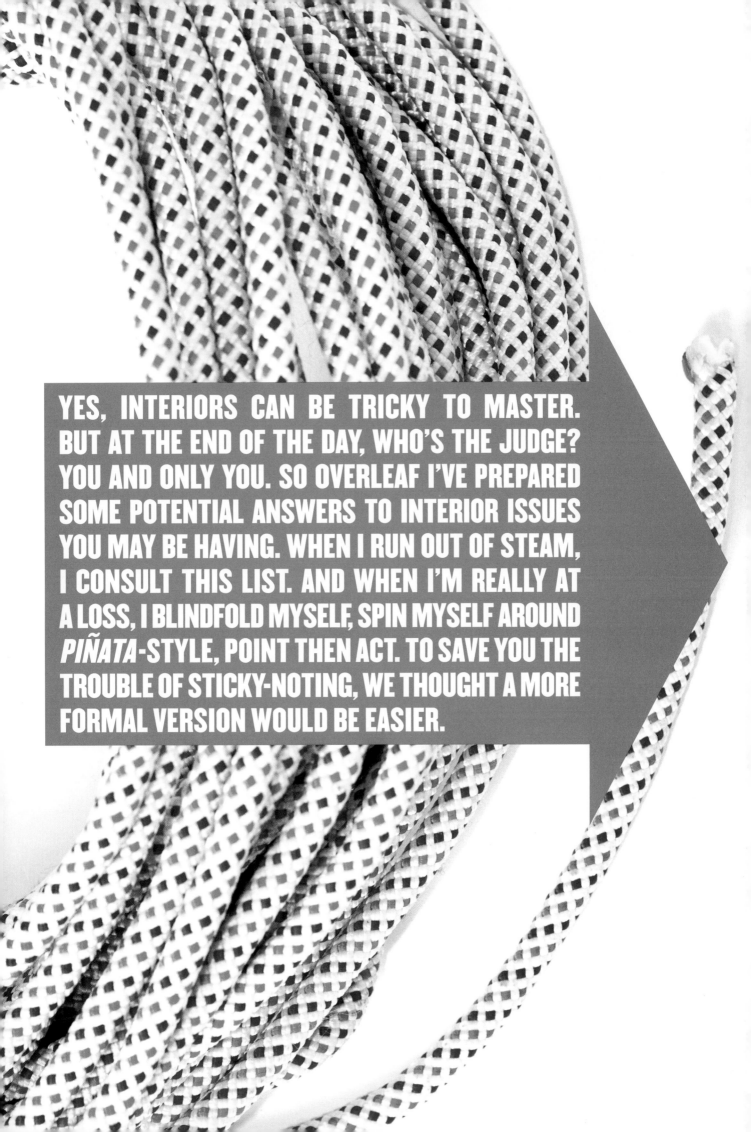

YES, INTERIORS CAN BE TRICKY TO MASTER. BUT AT THE END OF THE DAY, WHO'S THE JUDGE? YOU AND ONLY YOU. SO OVERLEAF I'VE PREPARED SOME POTENTIAL ANSWERS TO INTERIOR ISSUES YOU MAY BE HAVING. WHEN I RUN OUT OF STEAM, I CONSULT THIS LIST. AND WHEN I'M REALLY AT A LOSS, I BLINDFOLD MYSELF, SPIN MYSELF AROUND *PIÑATA*-STYLE, POINT THEN ACT. TO SAVE YOU THE TROUBLE OF STICKY-NOTING, WE THOUGHT A MORE FORMAL VERSION WOULD BE EASIER.

WHEN IN DOUBT, GO FOR BENTWOOD CHAIRS.

The most successful colour schemes have a dominant colour and a subordinate colour.

When things go wrong, it can force you to create a new set of solutions even better than the first.

NEVER

hang a mirror opposite your dining table, unless you like talking to your family in the third person.

Citrus trees look great in zinc pots. Always.

Keep your drinking glasses upside down, preferably on felt. Nothing worse than a dusty glass of pinot!

WHEN PERSONALISING YOUR SPACE, START AS A PURIST AND LET IT EVOLVE.

My motto – 'Something old, something new, something rough, something smooth' – helps me control my love of clutter.

NEVER COVET YOUR NEIGHBOUR'S HOUSE (UNLESS HE'S CHRISTIAN LIAIGRE). HOUSES ARE ONLY OF VALUE WHEN THE PEOPLE INSIDE THEM ARE.

Dream about living in an enchanted house. It really does happen.

Believe in plenty of optimism and white paint. And encourage sunshine in all rooms.

To escape the cleaning doldrums, hide treats in the laundry. A surprise slab of peanut brittle is a great incentive, as is booking a late lunch date with a friend.

This manifesto can work in one of two ways. One – keep it Post-it noted for bursts of inspiration, words from the wise if you like. Two – close your eyes, think of your problem, let your fingers run over the pages, then stop and voilà – your finger is on the answer. Making a house beautiful can throw up some challenges, so sage advice, another opinion and humour are all important!

}

OVE

NIFESTO

Pose Kevin McCloud's perennial question: 'If you had more quality in your life, would you crave for less?'

If your kitchen is unrenovated, hide one super-nice thing in each yucky cupboard. Whenever you happen upon it you'll smile.

WHEN YOU REALISE YOU CAN'T AFFORD TO RENOVATE, DON'T PIN THE ARCHITECT'S AFTER-PICTURE ON YOUR NOTICE BOARD.

Even if something is expensive, it only has value if you love it.

Always be making plans.

BIG PLANS.

Barbie Dream House plans.

(Thank you, Jonathan Adler.)

MY FRIEND'S MOTHER USED TO FOLLOW US DOWN THE HALL WITH A BACK-VAC, REMOVING OUR FOOTPRINTS FROM THE CARPET. **If** you live with children, make your major pieces durable and the smaller pieces flexible. Then, the minute they're gone, get back in that glorious decorating chair.

The window is to the view what the frame is to the painting. Don't scrimp on your windows.

The bathroom is the only room where you're guaranteed to come into daily contact with the surfaces. This is why you're investing so much in the bathroom taps, tiles, bath and flooring.

If you do a good arrangement, take a photo! Sometimes you need to be reminded of what you did and how.

Buying stuff for stuff's sake can leave you with a short-term high but long-term hollowness. Buy things with a narrative, that tell you who made it, where and why.

Although nature conditions us to expect the darkest colour values at our feet, medium at eye level and lightest above us, you can fly in the face of this.

DON'T USE THE STRAIGHT-BACKED SEATING FROM THE 16TH CENTURY, WHEN NO ONE HAD TIME TO SIT DOWN.

COMFORT SHOULD OVERRIDE PROVIDENCE.

IGNORE URGES
TO PAINT ONE WALL
A FEATURE COLOUR.
Please.
Instead, turn your attention to the front door.

RESIST WHITE WALLS IN THE CLYDESDALE ROOMS – LAUNDRIES, HOME OFFICES, ETC. USE COLOUR INSTEAD.

When the whole house is in disarray, take solace in a meticulous linen press (see page 196).

If stuck when deciding on colours, choose one master – Nature.

TURN YOUR CLOCK RADIO TO THE SALSA STATION FOR A CHANGE.

Your home should be either underdressed or overdressed. Anything in between can be a yawn.

A mobile is a lot cheaper to replace than a chandelier, which can really hog the whole room with its twinkly look-at-me-ness.

IF YOU'RE INTO 'STUFF', ASK YOURSELF, 'IS THIS BEAUTIFUL OR IS IT PET RESCUE FOR CERAMIC DOG FIGURINES?'

The Best Movies *for*

HOUSE-PERVING

HERE ARE MY FAVOURITE MOVIES FOR HOUSE-PERVING –
TO ENJOY THE DÉCOR TO THE MAX, TURN ON THE MUTE,
SIT BACK AND DROOL!

AN AMERICAN IN PARIS
The best use of small space ever.

THE DARJEELING LIMITED
I want a bathroom like the one on the train!

PILLOW TALK
Incredible decorating for a Kelly Wearstler–style bachelorette pad.

NEW YORK, I LOVE YOU
Six fine opportunities to see some of the Big Apple's most covetable
lofts and apartments. (For more, see the 'Houses I Love' section).

THE COOK, THE THIEF,
HIS WIFE AND HER LOVER
The play of dark and light is inspired.

ADDICTED TO LOVE
One of Nancy Meyers' finest.

THE ROYAL TENENBAUMS
Giraffe wallpaper anyone? And a corner brownstone? Oh yes, please!

Stylist's Glossary

MOST OF THE TIME I FEEL LIKE I HAVE NO WORDS FOR WHAT I'VE SEEN.
SO THEN SOMETIMES I MAKE UP WORDS FOR WHAT I'M SEEING AND DOING.
WHILE THIS IS BY NO MEANS A DEFINITIVE LIST, HERE ARE SOME OF THE
BETTER ONES THAT CAN BE USED IN NON-STYLING LIFE.

Zhoosh
You know this one, and it feels
good when you do it well.

Put the icing on
Finish it off, bring it home

×2
Double the effort – it's only halfway there.

Wind me
As in 'Take my breath away'.

Thesaurus it
Give me something like it, but not it.

Samla
Swedish for 'assemble', used to suggest the
product is a flat pack so if you have no time
to put it together, don't bother getting it.

Bon
Can be used singularly or often
multiple times. So good, good, good!

Dragon-fruity
It's not to everyone's taste, but possibly
overlooked, like a the flavour and
appearance of a dragon fruit.

Semifreddo
You're half cold on the idea, not yet
convinced – it could go either way.

Switzerland
When you do two options
to cover your bases.

Cordialled
To mean that an image got watered down.

What would John say?
This refers to a more botanical set-up
and asks if it's good enough to win the
approval of John Derian, the master.

Aeropelican
As in 'You're not flying Aeropelican'
(a regional, small airline), so make it
bigger and more fabulous.

Cred-itorial
Given the staggering amount of free-of-
charge information online these days, print
(i.e. books and magazines) remains queen
bee for genuinely credible information.
(Made up by Rennae Long, who works
with me! Thanks, RL!)

Credits

page ii
Photography by Sam Mackie, styling by Megan Morton, book by Nicholas Jones.

page viii
Betsy's House (see also pages 54–59); photography by Jason Busch, styling by Megan Morton; Marilyn Monroe artwork by Bert Stern.

Houses I Love

pages 5–79
Photography by Jason Busch, styling by Megan Morton.

pages 80–85
Photography by Anson Smart, photography by Megan Morton.

pages 5–9 Nigel, New York
Custom-made furniture by Nick Rogers from Primary Limited; artworks and an unknown Iranian artist.

pages 10–15 The Hartes, Sydney
Kitchen designed by Marion Hall Best; page 12 wallpaper is Josef Frank's Vårklocka in white, available from Just Scandinavian, New York.

pages 16–19 Hannah, Sydney
House designed by Hannah Tribe of Tribe Studio Architects, built by Jason Sewell from JLS Constructions; floors are highly durable and very cost-effective 15 mm compressed-fibre cement boards.

pages 19–23 The Barnums, Sydney
House designed by Terry Bail from Archology, built by Charlie and Joey Jnaid of SJ Developments, interior design by Lissa Barnum from Barnum Group.

pages 24–27 Ari, Brisbane
Architecture by Paul Owen and Stuart Vokes from Owen and Vokes; page 25 untitled paintings by Ari Athans; top left page 26 artworks by (bottom left to right) Beci Orpin, Ari Athans, David Bromley, Ari Athans (sandstone sculpture), Marina Strocchi and (top left to right) Ben Frost, Adam Lester, Max Athans Kassulke (Ari's son!), Adam Lester (ship), Darcy Clarke; bottom right page 26 untitled fabric installation by Ari.

pages 28–31 Georgie, Sydney
Grilles, doors and sconces forged by ironmonger Carmelo based in part on examples Georgie had seen around Lake Como.

pages 32–37 Vanessa, New York
Notes and art from friends, notably artworks by David Band, Roland Bello, Frédéric Lagrange, Shane Powers, Mary Matson, Confetti Systems, Susie

Cushner, Petrina Tinslay and Jason Polan; furniture by Mitchell Gold + Bob Williams, Ochre, Global Table, Blu Dot and West Elm; top right page 35 (and background page 33) bottles by Ochre, little gold hat by Confetti Systems, leg artwork by Frédéric Legrange, egg artwork by Susie Cushner, plate and cup artwork by David Band, beaded wire figure a Johannesburg artisan find, pirate flag by John Derian.

pages 38–41 Victus, Melbourne
House designed by Stephen Javens of Buro Architects, interior design by Kerry Phelan; pages 38 and 40 stairwell graffiti decal by Julia Gorman; bottom right page 40 black sculpture by Clement Meadmore; top right page 40 portraits on floor by Lewis Miller.

pages 42–49 Richard, Montauk, NY
Richard personally thanks 'Lena Kuffner for her design inspiration, Amy Wilson for her green thumbs and Jonathan Ferrantelli for being everything all the time'.

pages 45–53 Kids & chickens, Southern Highlands
Wallpaper by Kate Banazi; top left page 52 cushion by Beci Orpin.

pages 54–59 Betsy, New York
Architecture by Beyhan Karahan & Associates, Daniel McKay general contractor and project manager, built by Walker Ridge Construction, interior architecture by Messana O'Rorke; furniture from West Elm, eBay, 1stdibs and Beall & Bell; Marilyn Monroe artwork page 55 by Andy Warhol; moth artwork top right page 56 by Joseph Scheer.

pages 60–65 Ivan & Mary, New York
This unique workspace has been populated by Ivan and Mary's own work and wares.

pages 66–69 Julia, Melbourne
Original architecture by Wood Marsh; top left page 68 artwork by Imants Tillers; bottom page 68 artworks by Tony Clark (far left on stool), Fiona Somerville (centre), Lewis Miller (right), Joanne Ritson (far right above stool); top page 69 artworks by (clockwise from top left) Carolyn Eskdale, Sarah Ritson, Jenny Holzer, Joanne Ritson and Andrew Hurle.

pages 70–73 Shan, Brisbane
Top page 70 figures on chest *Listening to Light Over Water* by David Tucker (John Gordon Gallery), above figures *Mountain Devil* by Kathleen Petyarre (Delmore Gallery), behind chair *Kapitjukla (Waterhole)* by Molly Tjami (Mimili Maku Arts); bottom page 70 artworks (clockwise from top left) *When I Was a Little Girl* by Sharon Green, *I Dream of*

Many Things by Tom D., plate by Trixie Delicious of Vandalised Vintage, and book carving *White-Fronted Honeyeater* by Kylie Stillman (Utopia Art Sydney); painting page 71 by Sally Gabori; pages 71 and 72 Arne Jacobsen Series 7 chairs in brights; pages 72–73 artworks *Country Billabong* by Janie Sandy, *Waterfall* by Geoff Vlasie, *Bush Country* and *Lake Mary* by Maureen Thompson, *Flying Fox* by Myra Rory, *Message Stick Diwurruwurra* by Nancy McDinny, *Women Collecting Bush Medicine* by Lindy Brodie, *Mission Party* by Yondee Hansen.

pages 74–79 Annie, Sydney
Annie did the interiors, landscape exteriors and everything else in between; page 74 Marilyn Monroe limited print from Andy Warhol; page 78 painted canvas reproduction of 'Sight' from *The Lady and the Unicorn* tapestry series, circa 1500, held by the Musée de Cluny in Paris.

pages 80–85 Our house, Sydney
Carpentry by Jakes Clifton; top left page 80 *It's Beautiful Here* by Tara Maynes; bottom right page 80 artwork behind lamp by Edit; page 81 large artwork *Snow* by Rachel Castle; bottom right page 82 rosette by Tara Badcock of Paris + Tasmania; centre left page 82 artworks are junk shop finds, except for schnauzer wall tile from Best in Park top right of clock; bottom right page 82 artworks by Lisa Cooper (top), John Derian (bottom), Cameroon juju hat from Tractor Home over fireplace; top left page 83 plates by Bleus d'Ailleurs, artworks Rachel Castle (top), David Band (bottom left), Brydie Brown (bottom right, porcelain-dipped glove); top right page 83 artwork by Anna Mackrell (top), Maria Villa (bottom left), David Band (bottom right); bottom right page 84 heart artwork by Rachel Castle; bottom left page 83 children's portraits by Michelle Ball; page 85 garland by Rachel Castle, artworks by David Band.

Things I Love

pages 86–121
Photography by Sam Mackie, styling by Megan Morton, except where otherwise noted below.

page 89 'Nanna flowers'
Bottom left photographed by Elsa Hutton.

page 91 'Clean slates'
Top right photographed in the Barnum House (see also pages 20–23).

page 93 'Act with open heart'
Photography by Jason Busch, styling by Megan Morton; bottom left rosette made by Tara Badcock of Paris + Tasmania.

THANK YOU,
SAMANTHA MACKIE.*
I LOVED
EVERY MINUTE OF
WORKING WITH YOU —
ESPECIALLY THE
FOOD-RELATED JOBS!

* SEE OVER AT SAMANTHAMACKIE.BLOGSPOT.COM.AU

...and thanks to

JASON BUSCH (ROOMIMAGES.COM)
ANSON SMART, SOPHIE THÉ, EVI OETOMO,
NICOLA YOUNG AND JULIE GIBBS,
WHO PUTS THE LIGHT INTO LANTERN.
YOU'RE ALL OUTSTANDING
IN YOUR FIELD.

Index

First published in 2012 by the Penguin Group (Australia)
707 Collins Street, Melbourne, Victoria 3008, Australia
(a division of Pearson Australia Group Pty Ltd)

This edition published in Great Britain in 2013
by Conran Octopus Limited,
a part of Octopus Publishing Group,
Endeavour House, 189 Shaftesbury Avenue,
London WC2H 8JY
www.octopusbooks.co.uk

An Hachette UK Company
www.hachette.co.uk

Text copyright © Megan Morton 2012

Design and illustrations by Evi O © Penguin Group (Australia)
Front cover photography by Jason Busch, styling by Megan Morton,
    bottles by Ochre, little gold hat by Confetti Systems, leg artwork
    by Frédéric Legrange, egg artwork by Susie Cushner, plate and
    cup artwork by David Band
Front endpaper photography by Jason Busch, styling by Megan Morton
Inside front endpaper photography by Sam Mackie, styling by
    Sophie Thé, wooden house cut-out by Koskela
Back cover photography by Sam Mackie, styling by Sophie Thé
Back endpaper photography by Sam Mackie, styling by Megan
    Morton, painting by Stephanie Blake, rosette by Tara Badcock
    of Paris + Tasmania
Inside back endpaper photography by Sam Mackie,
    styling by Megan Morton
Author photography by Anson Smart
Typeset in Times Ten and Gotham by Evi O

All rights reserved. Without limiting the rights under copyright
reserved above, no part of this publication may be reproduced,
stored in or introduced into a retrieval system, or transmitted, in
any form or by any means (electronic, mechanical, photocopying,
recording or otherwise), without the prior written permission of
both the copyright owner and the above publisher of this book.

The moral right of the author has been asserted

British Library Cataloguing-in-Publication Data.
A catalogue record for this book is available from the British
Library.

ISBN 978 1 84091 625 6

Colour separation by Splitting Image Colour Studio Pty Ltd,
    Clayton, Victoria
Printed in China

The author and publisher would like to thank the people and
companies credited on pages 210–11 for allowing us to reproduce
their material in this book. In some cases we were unable to contact
the copyright owners; we would appreciate hearing from any
copyright holders not acknowledged here, so that we can properly
acknowledge their contribution when this book is reprinted.